NORTHEAST FOUNDATION FOR CHILDREN, INC.

Sammy and His Behavior Problems

Stories and Strategies from a Teacher's Year

CALTHA CROWE

The stories in this book are true. However, in order to respect the privacy of students, their names and many identifying characteristics have been changed.

ISBN 978-1-892989-31-4

Library of Congress Control Number: 2009932501

Cover and book design by Helen Merena

Thanks to the children whose drawings grace these pages.

Northeast Foundation for Children, Inc.
85 Avenue A, Suite 204
P. O. Box 718
Turners Falls, MA 01376-0718

800-360-6332
www.responsiveclassroom.org

15 14 13 12 11 10   7 6 5 4 3 2 1

Printed on recycled paper

To Sammy and his family

❖

Contents

Introduction

Every year we teachers have some students who present challenges to themselves, their classmates, and to us. Sometimes it's the student who refuses to do schoolwork and wanders around the classroom distracting others. Sometimes it's the child who shouts out in group lessons and makes noises as she walks across the room, providing a raucous sound-track to our days. At other times it's the child who takes others' possessions and insults classmates. It's our responsibility to teach these children, helping them get better at managing their behaviors and become effective students, while still meeting the learning needs of their less obviously demanding classmates. Our challenge is to be there for each and every one of our students each and every day.

My book *Solving Thorny Behavior Problems: How Teachers and Students Can Work Together* offers strategies that a teacher might use when children persistently misbehave. As I wrote it, I often thought of a former student of mine, "Sammy." I used every strategy offered in *Thorny* and more with Sammy. Over time, these strategies helped him grow in both the social and academic arenas. After I finished writing *Thorny*, I decided that it might be helpful to teachers if I told the story of Sammy's year.

If you've read *Solving Thorny Behavior Problems*, you'll find some familiar strategies in this book. I hope reading about Sammy will help you gain a more nuanced picture of which strategy a teacher might use when, and why. I hope you'll gain new insights about how the strategies fit together. I hope you'll see how I used failures as well as successes to revise and refine the ways I worked with Sammy. I also hope you'll notice how the strategies I used with the whole class created an atmosphere of calm and respect, giving Sammy the environment he needed to become more calm and respectful himself.

Although this book tells the story of one particular child in one particular school, it contains some universal good practices that apply to the teaching of any child with challenging behavior in any classroom. These are practices that I learned from wise colleagues or discovered myself through trial and error. Though I didn't use them perfectly every day—no teacher can—I anchored my teaching with them the year I taught Sammy, and every year. Some of the most important of these universal practices are:

- Genuinely liking the child (there's something to like in every child; we just have to look to see it)

- Stopping often to observe the child

- Having genuine conversations with the child; listening more, talking less

- Trying to see things from the child's point of view; taking that point of view seriously even if it differs from our own

- Holding other children to the high standard of respecting all classmates, including ones who may be a little "different"

- Offering a developmentally appropriate, engaging curriculum (yes, this is indeed possible even in an age of testing and standards)

- Understanding, and helping the class understand, "fairness": building an effective learning community is not about giving every child the same thing, but giving every child what he or she needs

There is one final most-important practice: forming a strong student-teacher relationship. The bedrock of my work with Sammy was our relationship. As I came to know and appreciate him, we were able to work together to solve some of his difficulties in school. As my relationship with Sammy grew, so did his relationships with the other students in our class. Friendships with peers did not come easily to him, but our class worked hard on becoming an accepting community, supporting all of the students, and by the end of the year Sammy was able to say "I made some friends."

The story of my year with Sammy is told from my point of view. Events described are events that I observed or participated in. However, it takes a whole school to work effectively with a child with significant behavioral and academic challenges. Our administrators created an adult community where the staff felt safe sharing our ups and downs and our successes and failures with each other. Sammy's teachers from previous years shared effective strategies as well as strategies that had been less successful. Art, music, and physical education teachers as well as paraprofessionals who had known Sammy for several years provided invaluable suggestions. Special educators and our school psychologist shared insights based on their specialized knowledge and understanding. Sammy attended a lunchtime social skills group led by our school psychologist. All these supports and the classroom's social and academic curricula combined to help Sammy grow.

What about Sammy's privacy?

As I contemplated this project, my first concern was how to write such a book in a way that would honor Sammy and his family. First, I spoke with them, explaining what I wanted to do and why. Together, they then discussed their thoughts and feelings about such a book. Ultimately, Sammy and his parents decided that they'd like to help teachers work effectively with children who have behavior challenges, but that they wanted Sammy's privacy to be protected. I myself saw preserving his privacy as a paramount goal. "Sammy," of course, is a made-up name. I've also changed many details that might identify him.

On the other hand, the events that I describe, both Sammy's behaviors and my responses, really happened. My goal was to tell the story of his year truthfully, preserving the essence of our year together, our ups and downs, our goals met and unmet. Sammy's family and I hope that by reading the story of his year, you'll gain new ideas about how to work with your own "Sammy."

BEGINNINGS

The First Six Weeks of School

Chapter One

Getting to Know Sammy

It's the morning of the second day of school. The new third grade students sit in a circle on the floor. Glancing around, I see well-scrubbed children, shining with that beginning-of-school look.

I bring out a "magic shawl," beneath which is hidden the learning material I'm about to introduce. I use this method to heighten intrigue and student engagement. The children are curious, eager to know what's under the shawl. They're using their first-days-of-school best behavior though, keeping their bodies and their wiggles mostly under control. We're all feeling the power of new beginnings.

I unveil the Cuisenaire® Rods, colorful and inviting. I ask the children what they know about this material and how they think they might use it. Paulina suggests building a tower. Max suggests creating a series of equal groups. Juan mentions that in second grade they made "staircases" with the rods. The children listen carefully. I explain that they'll each get a chance to try out classmates' ideas, using just a few rods each. They're excited.

Walking around the circle, I carefully give each child a small handful of rods. As I come to Sammy, I hand him a small assortment, similar to his classmates'. In a flash Sammy darts his hands into the bin on my arm, pulling out an additional big double handful for himself.

Quietly, I hold out my hand for Sammy to return his double handful. "Just a few each, Sammy," I remind him calmly. As quickly as he had grabbed the rods, Sammy throws them at my face. Rods rain down. The look on Sammy's face shows that he's as surprised as I am. His classmates look stunned.

We all have students who present challenges to their classmates, themselves, and to us. Sammy was such a child. This Cuisenaire Rod incident was Sammy's first major display of teacher defiance that year. There would be many more. As the year went on, I came to see that Sammy's behavior largely grew out of his impulsiveness combined with deep passions and a gripping need to put his ideas into action. Helping Sammy gain control of his behavior so that he could learn—and so the rest of the class could learn—would make that year both challenging and rewarding.

Like all children, Sammy was a complex individual. There was a lot to him besides his challenging behaviors. Even before school started, I got a glimpse of his charms as well as his behaviors that got in the way.

"Dear Third Grade Teacher, My name is Sammy and I am passionate about history."

In August I clean, organize, and prepare for the students who will be walking through the door in just two weeks. I gather information about the children, preparing myself mentally for the personalities and likely interactions that will make up our group.

As I peruse Sammy's records, I notice phrases such as "ADD," "extremely bright," even "gifted." In Sammy's second grade portfolio is a letter that he wrote to me, his as yet unidentified next year's teacher.

"Dear Third Grade Teacher, My name is Sammy and I am passionate about history," the letter begins. "Have you heard about the Iroquois League of five nations? Will we learn about it in third grade?" His personality is coming through already. I make a mental note to borrow some additional age-appropriate history books from the public library to add to our classroom collection.

Sammy's letters are large and shaky, the lines wandering over the page. I wonder, "Are his ideas tumbling out so quickly that his handwriting can't keep up?"

Sammy's second grade teacher stops by the classroom. "I hear you have Sammy," she says. "He just can't sit still. He loves to read. Usually I let him sit and read by himself during Morning Meeting and whole-group lessons. He can't listen in those settings."

I'm always glad for information that might help me with my teaching, and I have a lot of respect for Sammy's second grade teacher. Nonetheless, it's hard for me to imagine Sammy as a true member of our community if he doesn't join in at whole-group times. I accept the second grade teacher's information while promising myself to at least try including Sammy in group activities. I realize this goal might not be easily achieved.

As the days before school race past, I talk with the school nurse and the PE, music, and other special subject teachers, as some of them have known my new students for multiple years. I'm beginning to piece together a still-blurry picture of Sammy as a bright, inquisitive child who is always on the move.

Who is still seven in this class? Who is firmly eight?

As part of my preparation, I consider the children's ages and likely developmental characteristics, so important in understanding them and setting appropriate expectations. I begin by listing the students in birthday order. Who is still seven? Who is firmly eight, with a birthday last winter or spring? Who is about to turn nine?

Keeping a list like this often helps me maintain patience with the constant physical aches and pains of a seven-year-old or the single-minded focus on fairness of a nine-year-old. I reread sections of *Yardsticks: Children in the Classroom Ages 4–14* by Chip Wood to review the characteristics of seven-, eight-, and nine-year-olds.

Glass taxes, square roots, colonial history: Brimming over with interests

It's the day before school, and the children are coming for "meet the teacher," an annual tradition at our school. Name tags are laid out on a table, and a message on the message board asks, "What are you looking forward to in third grade?"

The children arrive, some shy and hanging back, others boisterous and eager to connect with friends old and new. Sammy walks through the door with his mother and older brother. He's carrying a thick book about colonial history under his arm.

He looks right at me, smiles, and starts to announce facts about colonial times. "Did you know that in the early 1800s people had to pay a glass tax if their homes had more than ten windows?" he asks me. I smile and express genuine interest, happy to meet him and to begin to connect.

I show Sammy the message board and urge him to think about what he's looking forward to in third grade. "Well," he says, "I'm looking forward to lots of things. It's hard to choose. Will we learn about history? Will we learn about square roots? How do I know what third grade is going to be like?" Seemingly exhausted by the choice, he suddenly writes "Learning" as his response on the message board.

I ask Sammy to show other kids how to answer the message. I have a feeling from my research over the past couple of weeks that Sammy's going to need a specific job to help him connect with classmates.

Five minutes later I look over at the message board and notice Sammy grabbing the marker out of a student's hand, saying, "No, it's not your turn yet." I make a mental note to give Sammy more direct instruction next time about what helping other kids with the morning message looks and sounds like.

For now, I go over to Sammy and his classmates to intervene, suggesting that Sammy make a name tag for his locker in the hall.

Here, everyone sits with everyone else; everyone works with everyone else

The all-important first day of school is finally here. The children arrive, in surging waves as their school busses unload. I greet them with the Human Treasure Hunt for finding and talking with all classmates.

Who can you find who lived in another country last year? Who loves hot dogs? Who speaks Japanese at home? The questions are both generic and specific. Lots of children might love hot dogs, but only one speaks Japanese at home. Thus I've planned things so that everyone will greet Mitsuke, who's new in our school.

Who loves history? is also on the list, as I want to make sure children begin to connect with Sammy. I've heard that making friends has been hard for him in the past, and this will gently nudge him in the right direction.

In this classroom, children sit in table groups based on playing cards they draw from the well-shuffled pack in my hand. Here, everyone sits with everyone else, and everyone works with everyone else. Throughout the year we'll discuss why it's important to get to know all members of our classroom community, and children will pick lunch partners—"someone you don't know very well."

The underlying message, implied through our activities and stated directly, is that everyone is a part of this group. Children such as Sammy, who seem a little different to their classmates, can be excluded, teased, even bullied. It's the teacher's job to set up an environment where such behaviors are clearly unacceptable.

Our first Morning Meeting

We gather in a circle each morning for a Morning Meeting, a twenty- to thirty-minute period when children greet and get to know each other, practice social and academic skills through fun activities, and set a positive tone for the day ahead.

To launch our first Morning Meeting, I say to the class, "Every day we'll start our day with a Morning Meeting. What kind of meetings have you been to?" I'm trying to assess their knowledge and expectations.

"Last year we had a Morning Meeting every day," says Lori. "We played games. It was fun."

"We also said 'good morning,'" adds Paul.

"I go to town meetings with my mom," shares Sammy. "There's an agenda. They talk about the topics on the agenda. People listen to each other."

Next I lead them in establishing some meeting expectations that will allow us to have meetings that are enjoyable and helpful for everyone. When I ask for suggestions, Sammy's hand goes up right away. "Listen to each other the way they do at town meetings," he says. I write "Listen" on a small whiteboard I've placed near the meeting area.

Other students suggest additional meeting rules, mostly things they picked up from previous grades. "Sit in the circle," "Raise your hand to speak," "Control your body" all make the list.

I go on to model greeting a classmate, the first thing we'll be doing every day in Morning Meeting. After getting a few students to demonstrate this procedure after me, we go around the circle for real, each child greeting a neighbor so everyone gets greeted by name.

Prepped by the careful modeling, most of the children are friendly and attentive to their peers. Sammy, however, is rolling on the floor by the time the greeting has gone a quarter of the way around the circle. Today I let this behavior go. His rolling is quiet, and the other children look like they can still focus on the greeting. I'm still getting to know Sammy and want to watch and learn. Based on information I've gleaned from colleagues, I'm actually surprised that he was able to listen to the greeting at all.

When the greeting completes its circuit, we're ready to share the information that children have gathered about their new classmates from the Human Treasure Hunt.

"Why is it important to listen as classmates tell what they've learned about each other?" I ask.

"So that we can find out about each other," Michele says.

"Because it's polite," suggests Jerry.

"Yes," I say. "In this class we listen to each other respectfully." My goal is to immediately set the expectation that every group member deserves our attention and respect.

The children enthusiastically take turns reporting on the results of their search. They tell about the many students who like hot dogs, the one class-mate who speaks Japanese at home, and the one who loves to play baseball.

Sammy's still rolling. His legs are under the easel chart stand, one foot beating steadily against the leg of the stand. If I allow it to escalate, his be-havior will become disruptive. I touch his foot gently, and he stops the beat-ing.

We've been sitting for nearly fifteen minutes now, a long time for chil-dren just back from summer vacation. So we switch gears and play a round of When the Big Wind Blows, an activity that gets everyone up and mov-ing. Now that we're in motion, Sammy joins in happily. I take note, think-ing about how I'll handle Sammy's behavior tomorrow in our second Morning Meeting.

Shared laughter helps us begin to bond

The children are writing letters to me about themselves, their families, their interests, and what they're looking forward to in third grade. I have students do this first-day activity almost every year.

As the children write, I circulate, stopping at each child for brief but personal conversation. I comment on Jenny's description of her cat and Garret's fascination with bears. I ask about siblings and favorite television shows. I smile, listen, and look at each child: all behaviors that begin to build connections. A strong, positive teacher-student relationship is so important to a child's school success.

"Ms. Crowe, Ms. Crowe, what's purple and 5000 miles long?" Sammy bounces up and down on his toes while waiting for me to answer. "I don't know," I answer. "What?"

"The grape wall of China," he crows with excitement. Our shared laughter helps us begin to bond.

It's important that I find what's likeable in each student. I need to like students in order to be a good teacher to them. It's not about pretending to like them, which they would surely see through, but genuinely liking them. I try to see things from their point of view so I might understand what they're thinking and feeling. I make it a priority to listen to them. I try to find something we have in common, whether it's loving to read or being slow to wake up in the morning. All these things help me like the students. Often it's the child who's initially a little hard to like, the one for whom I had to make extra effort, that I become most attached to as the year goes on.

Our second Morning Meeting

Day two. It's time for our second Morning Meeting of the year. I know from yesterday that sitting in the circle listening to classmates is going to be hard for Sammy.

I whisper quietly and privately to him, "How can I help you listen to the other kids?"

His face wrinkles with distress. "I don't know. It's hard for me."

"I wondered about that," I reply in a nonjudgmental tone. "Sit next to me and I'll help you."

The strategy of "proximity" is a time-honored teacher move to encourage attention in children who have a tough time sitting still and listening. As I use it with Sammy, I'm also establishing that I can be his ally around things that are hard.

By the time the greeting makes it halfway around the circle, Sammy has crawled into my lap. The physical contact calms him, and he listens almost the entire time his classmates are greeting each other.

"You did it," I whisper to him after the meeting. "You listened for most of the greeting." In reinforcing this positive behavior, I'm careful to name what he really did do—listened for most of the greeting portion of the meeting—rather than what I might have wished he did—listened for the whole Morning Meeting. In any relationship, honesty is important.

From my journal, September 4:

There's a lot to like in Sammy. He has passionate interests, a sense of humor, a sunny smile, and a way with words. We'll be fine as long as I don't take his out-of-control behavior personally. Those behaviors aren't about me, although I know that my own behaviors might exacerbate his. If I get wound up, his intensity will increase. My job is to be his ally in gaining more control of himself. I'll do that best if I stay calm and positive.

Fair isn't the same as equal

One of my colleagues, a special educator, joins our class for a Morning Meeting. Later in the day, as we discuss what she noticed, she mentions how active Sammy was during the meeting. "It might help him to have some therapy putty to manipulate during the meeting. Lots of kids concentrate better when they have something to do with their hands," she suggests. "Therapy putty might help Marie, too," she adds. Marie is a student in the class who has a diagnosis of autism and often has difficulty focusing during group sessions.

I ask Sammy what he thinks. "Sammy, would it help you pay attention in Morning Meeting if you had something to do with your hands?"

"Yup," he says. "I've had putty before. You can roll it or pinch it."

"You're right, Sammy, putty is for rolling and pinching only. Let's try it tomorrow," I say. "Mrs. O'Rourke said that she'd get some for you and for Marie."

Later on, the class sits together for a brief end-of-the-day closing circle. I use the opportunity to explain why Sammy and Marie, and no doubt many other students at different points in the year, will get to have some things or get to do some things that not every member of the class will. "We all need different things in order to be successful," I say to the class. "Pua needs glasses in order to read. What are some other things that individual students need in order to be successful?"

Hands go up. "When I broke my foot, I needed crutches," says Jerry.

"Last year I needed reading help from Mrs. Lane," says Jenny.

"So," I say, "it would be pretty silly if we all wore glasses because Pua does, or if we all used crutches when Jerry did. In this class, things are fair. But fair doesn't always mean doing exactly the same thing. It means everyone getting what they need, as much as possible."

I continue, "What are some things that everyone needs?"

"Everyone needs the teacher to listen to them," says Michele.

"That's right," I say. "Part of being a fair teacher is that I do my very best to listen to everyone."

"Everyone needs a turn to share in Morning Meeting," adds Frankie.

"So in this class we're fair and we make sure that everyone gets to share once before anyone has a second turn," I confirm.

"Some of the things that we need are the same, but some are different," I summarize. "Tomorrow at Morning Meeting, Sammy and Marie are going to have some putty to roll and pinch. It's to help them pay attention. The putty is just for them because they need it."

I know this issue of fairness will come up throughout the year. I want to be explicit with students that they each need different things and that my job as their teacher is to provide each with what they need. Fair isn't always equal.

Friends

A major class project during the first days of school in our class is the creation of our classroom rules. This begins with the children individually articulating their goals for school this year—their "hopes and goals," as we call them. As a group they then come up with rules that will allow all of them to achieve their hopes and goals.

"THE KDS BOTHRD ME"

To get them thinking about their hopes and goals, I gather the children in a circle at the end of the first day of school. "My hope for our class this year is that it will be a safe and friendly place for everyone," I announce. "I hope that we will all treat each other with respect so that everyone feels comfortable."

I continue, "Tonight, for homework, you're each going to think about your hopes for third grade—what you wish for in your third grade year." I've prepared a worksheet with questions about experiences in second grade and hopes for third grade.

The children arrive the next morning with their worksheets complete. Sammy's is full of those wobbly letters. I can see that there have been plenty of erasures, as evidenced by several holes in the paper.

What did you like about second grade? REDNG wobbles across the page.

If you could change anything that you did in second grade, what would it be? THE KDS BOTHRD ME.

I'm learning a lot already, about Sammy's spelling with the many missing vowels, and about Sammy's perception of why things are sometimes hard for him.

"THE KDS BOTHRD ME" are strong words. Is this just his way of saying there were some classmates he didn't get along with? Or is he lumping all his second grade classmates together in one big "bothersome" group? I'm struck by what appears like very black-and-white thinking.

Sammy's hope and goal: "Maybe make friends"

The children spend parts of the next two days shaping their memories of last year and ideas for this year into well-articulated personal "hopes and goals" for third grade. They then copy these over in their best handwriting, illustrate them, and display the finished products. Paul wants to get better at math. Garret wants to get to know everyone in the class and make new friends. Jenny wants to become a better reader.

At the end of the two days, Sammy's rectangle on the bulletin board is empty. The cumulative steps—identifying one important goal, writing it neatly, and drawing an illustration—have felt overwhelming to him.

I meet with Sammy individually while others are doing their illustrations. "Sammy," I say, "what are you hoping for in third grade?"

Sammy mumbles, "I don't know. It's all too hard."

"Let's look at your worksheet."

Sammy fumbles in his folder and finds the paper crumpled up in the bottom of one of the folder pockets.

"I see here you say that kids bothered you. What might be a goal that would be related to changing that?"

"I don't know. Maybe make friends?" he suggests.

He is more able to meet the challenge of identifying a goal when we do it orally. I can see that writing is tough for him.

From hopes and goals to class rules

Once everyone has a hope and goal for third grade, we meet to begin our rule creation process. In introducing this task, I work in the children's goals. "If Paul wants to get better at math, if Sammy wants to make new friends, if Jenny wants to be a better reader, what rules will we need to make our classroom a place where they and everyone else can achieve their goals?"

The children partner chat and then share their ideas with the group. I write all of their suggestions on a chart. "Be friendly," "Do your work," and "Listen to the teacher" all go on the chart.

When Sammy adds "Don't kick kids," I say, "If we're not going to kick, what will we do?"

"Be safe with our feet," Juan suggests.

Over subsequent days we categorize the ideas on our chart, propose ways to consolidate all of our thoughts into a few encompassing rules that will be easy to remember, and finally come up with three "rules to live by":

- Respect and care for everyone.

- Listen and do your best work.

- Take care of our environment.

When I unveil these rules, the children cheer. They've worked hard to get these rules. There's a strong sense of ownership in the class—these are *our* rules.

This process of creating the rules has begun to bring us together as a community. Throughout the year I will be referring to these rules constantly, keeping them alive so our classroom will be a place that's safe for all the children. For Sammy in particular, the rule creation is a crucial step in establishing a climate that allows him to be a full community member, accepting of his classmates and accepted by them.

A miscalculation on my part

The children sit as I read *Chrysanthemum* by Kevin Henkes aloud to them. They're transfixed, and I'm enjoying reading a story that reinforces the importance of respecting each other's differences. When the story ends, we discuss strategies that the children used to follow the story, and that all good readers use when reading. "Were you making pictures in your mind? Were you asking yourself questions?" I ask.

Since Sammy's second grade teacher had told me that he has a hard time paying attention in group discussions, I had planned to keep him engaged by having him be the official class recorder during this and other whole-class lessons at the start of the year. "Sammy, will you record the kids' ideas on the whiteboard?" I ask.

"No, I don't want to," Sammy responds, head down, feet shuffling. Instead he hops like a bunny across the circle, nuzzles Frank with his nose, and hops behind the bookcase.

From my journal, September 5:

Before I met Sammy, with the infinite possibilities of August stretching in front of me, it seemed like such a good idea to have him record on the whiteboard during whole-class lessons. He'd be actively engaged, moving his body and reviewing the important concepts of the lesson. I hadn't taken into account the handwriting that I'd seen in Sammy's "Dear third grade teacher" letter. That was a clue, so plain now, that public writing was not going to be a comfortable activity for Sammy. I'll need to continue to pay attention to other strategies that might help Sammy attend. Our day two Morning Meeting experience leaves me optimistic that he can do it.

Driven to express his unique ideas

In the middle of a lesson on how to write about one's math thinking, Sammy gets up, walks across the circle and returns with scissors, paper, markers, and tape. He raises his hand. "I want to show the class another way to show your math thinking," he says.

He begins to create an elaborate paper sculpture with checkerboard charts and graphs. "I've been wanting to make this," he says.

The children look on, fascinated if a bit confused. I myself am not sure what Sammy is trying to show us. It is clear that some internal impulse is impelling him forward, fueling his need to create as he cuts and tapes.

I know that I need to respond to Sammy respectfully. My example will encourage the other students to treat Sammy with respect. I also need to keep the momentum of the lesson going. In lessons structured around students' ideas, it's important to accept all suggestions. It's also important to keep the pace moving and limit student rambling.

At my first opportunity, I thank Sammy and move on to the next student's thought about math writing.

Careful observation

Every morning Sammy arrives with a cheerful greeting, a story about something silly his brother did, or a history fact. He approaches me easily, smiling and conversing naturally. A new adult appears, and I notice Sammy telling that person a joke.

Approaching peers is another matter. He walks up to Garret and paws at him, making kitten noises. Garret gives him an annoyed look and says, "Stop that." Sammy mumbles and wanders away. I watch and learn.

He is active. I want him to be part of the group, to listen and share his ideas during whole-class lessons, to learn with us. I want him to feel that he belongs. He doesn't slide into the group easily though. To help, I've begun preparing him for each group lesson ahead of time and, building on the successes in Morning Meeting, I have him sit next to me during the lesson. I also quietly reinforce appropriate behavior with whispered comments. He's able to sit for at least part of each lesson as long as I do each of these steps.

But if I drop any of them, as I sometimes do, he loses focus and becomes disruptive. He hops across the circle and hides behind the bookcase, then crawls back out and over the other children. He pokes Max, who's trying to participate in the lesson. When Max doesn't respond, he thumps Max's head, metronome-like. I move Sammy away from Max, thinking about how to head off these incidents in the future.

Last week in the post office, I watched a four-year-old playing with his younger brother while their parent waited in line to mail a package. The four-year-old wanted his younger brother to notice the stamps displayed on the wall. To get his brother's attention, he beat on the child's head, hard and rhythmically. Sammy uses the same motion to get Max's attention.

I reflect on the similarity. Intellectually, Sammy often reminds me of a twelve-year-old. Socially, he sometimes reminds me of a four-year-old. Development is uneven like this. Often the child who is ahead in one area seems like a younger child in another. Framing Sammy's behavior issues this way helps me see the areas where he is going to need individual coaching.

Only a few days into school, I've already noticed so much about Sammy. He loves learning, especially about history. He has a great sense of humor. He has a gift for relating to adults. These are all strengths I can help him build on.

He wants to get along with peers, as evidenced by the fact that he reaches out to them, but he doesn't know how, as shown by what he does during the encounter. I can see by his enthusiasm that he wants to participate in class-room activities, but I have ample evidence that he also wants to follow his own desires, which sometimes clash with whole-class expectations.

As I step back and observe Sammy carefully, I come to know him as a person. The better I know him, the more empathy I feel for his joys and his challenges. Noticing how he relates to peers helps me devise strategies to help him build friendships. Noticing his characteristic learning style helps me teach him academics.

Coaching on how to approach other kids

After watching how awkwardly Sammy interacts with peers, I realize I have to preempt the pounding and pawing or classmates will start to avoid him.

As Sammy and I finish a conference about his independent reading, I bring up the issue of how to get a friend's attention.

"Sammy," I say, "I've noticed that sometimes you touch other kids when you want them to work or play with you." I use as neutral a word as possible— "touch"—while still describing the behavior clearly.

"Yup, I do," he answers. "That way they'll listen to me."

"Kids don't always like it when others touch them like that," I say.

"I can tell that you want them to listen to you and be your friend. Would you like some ideas about other ways to get kids to listen to you?"

"When I talked to Max about colonial America yesterday, he just turned away and started to talk with Manuel about baseball," Sammy begins to complain. "And today when I wanted Max to listen to me, he just turned away."

"What was Max doing when he turned away today?"

"Well … , he was listening to Lexi share her idea about the story," Sammy admits. He's referring to the whole-class lesson we were having.

"So we have a couple of challenges here," I say. "The first is how to know whether it's a good time to get someone to listen to you. The second is how to get someone to listen to you if it is a good time. How do you know if it's the right time to talk with a friend?"

"Well, it wasn't the right time when Max was listening to Lexi share with the class," he says.

"Why not?"

"You're not supposed to interrupt lessons or conferences."

"So, how will you know if it's an appropriate time?"

"I guess I could look first to see if it's a lesson or a conference," Sammy reflected.

"So when you want to talk with someone, you'll stop, look, and see if the person is busy with a lesson or with a conference, and if they're not then you'll go over to them." I name all the steps—stop, look, see—because I sense that Sammy needs them broken down and spelled out.

"What will you say to your friend if you want to talk with them?" I continue, thinking about Sammy's opening gambit about colonial America.

"I don't know. That's the problem. Not everyone is interested in colonial America. Some people are interested in dumb things like baseball."

I decide to leave the issue of listening to other people's interests for another time. I want to keep this discussion as simple as possible. "What about starting with a joke?" I suggest. "You know lots of jokes. That's often how you start a conversation with me."

"I could say 'Knock, knock,'" he suggests.

"OK, let's practice. Let's pretend I'm Max. You'll look to see if I'm listening to a lesson or if I'm in a conference. When you see that I'm not, then you'll look at me, hands to yourself, and say 'Knock, knock,'"

Sammy looks carefully all around the table. He checks his hands to make sure he's keeping them to himself. Then he says to me, "Knock, knock."

"Who's there?" I reply with a big smile.

"I think you've got it, Sammy," I say. "Next time, look, make sure the person's not busy, and if they aren't, say 'Knock, knock.'"

Our entire conversation took less than ten minutes. Sammy had learned a new skill about how to approach classmates. He'd need plenty of reminders and guided practice over the coming weeks, but we'd gotten a solid start.

At least a facsimile of partner work

I have students work in pairs a lot at the beginning of the year. This suits them developmentally, as many of them are seven or newly eight at the beginning of third grade; children this age tend to focus inward and have difficulty with the compromising that's involved in working with a small group. Later in the year, when they're older, we'll do more group work. For now, pair work is a good way for them to collaborate.

Today, at the end of the first week of school, I begin teaching the children how to work with a partner. I model "buzzing" about a book with a classmate, then guide the children in practicing this before sending them off to buzz with partners I had planned ahead of time.

Some of these pairings seemed quite obvious. Garret and Jenny both love animals and read books with somewhat simplified text and vocabulary. Mitsuke and Robert are both strong readers who will inspire each other to read new books and new authors. I puzzled over a partner for Sammy, deciding in the end that since Paul and Sammy are both interested in history, I'd give that duo a try.

The children scatter around the classroom with their new partners. Within minutes they are happily buzzing about their books, all except Sammy. As Paul tells Sammy about his historical fiction, *Journey to America,* Sammy turns somersaults on the floor and chirps like a chipmunk. I walk over to them.

"What's going on?" I ask.

"I listened to Sammy, but Sammy's not listening to me," Paul complains.

"I'm not interested in immigration in the 1900s," Sammy mutters. "I don't like fiction, and that book's about girls," he adds with disgust.

"You still need to be courteous to Paul," I reply. "Look at him and listen to him the way we practiced." All the while I'm thinking, "This isn't working."

The next day I try partnering Sammy with Marie. She prefers to read nonfiction, and her special education paraprofessional is in the classroom during reading time, so she provides adult support to help Sammy meet behavioral expectations. With supervision, Sammy is acquiescent but lacking in engagement.

From my journal, September 6:

I can see lots of reasons that partner work isn't easy for Sammy. He's seven, the youngest student in our class. The developmental characteristics of his age conspire against happy partner work. Also, he follows his own inner directives. Listening to a partner's ideas is not in his current repertoire of skills.

I could give up on partner work for Sammy, conclude that it's just too hard for him at this time. But if I did that, he would stand out even more, working alone while others pair up. I can't do that. I want to help bring Sammy into the group. I think I'll continue to have Sammy participate in at least a facsimile of partner work.

A fortress of books, a cascade of pop-ups

If children have favorite books from home or the public library, I encourage them to bring them in to share with the class. Children usually bring one book or, at most, two. Sammy arrives every morning pulling a huge duffle bag behind him like a reluctant dog on a leash. He unpacks, piling his books under and around the table area he shares with three other students. The volumes begin to slide into their work areas. I'm wondering if his fortress of books makes him feel more secure.

Throughout the day, whether during official classroom downtimes or because he's lost focus on his work, Sammy channels some of his endless energy into creating three-dimensional scenes of important events in history. During Quiet Time after lunch, when children are reading or drawing, Sammy is unobtrusively folding his drawing paper, turning it into a historical scene. Children are arriving in the morning, and Sammy is off in a corner, cutting and pasting. His readiness to make himself at home in this classroom is a sign that he's feeling comfortable here. But these scenes, or "pop-ups," as he calls them, cascade into his tablemates' work area. They're starting to complain.

"Sammy, your pop-ups cover the whole table": Conflict resolution with tablemates

It's my job to protect the tablemates from the cascading pop-ups and to protect Sammy's need to feel safe and express his creativity. So rather than simply telling Sammy to stop the dioramas, I take the opportunity to coach the group in conflict resolution so they might arrive at a solution that meets everyone's needs. This will also help the tablemates practice assertion and help Sammy practice listening. I join their table and begin.

"Pua, you said something to me this morning about Sammy's pop-ups," I begin. "Tell Sammy what you told me. Look at him while you tell him," I add. Third graders are good at telling the teacher how they were wronged. My goal here is to teach them how to tell each other, directly and respectfully.

"Sammy, listen carefully because I'm going to ask you to restate what Pua said when she's finished." Sammy needs a pre-alert about what's expected. Otherwise there's no way he'll listen.

Pua takes a deep breath and looks right at Sammy. "Sammy, I don't have room to open my notebook at our table. Your pop-ups cover the whole table."

"OK, Sammy, now it's your turn. Tell Pua what you heard her say."

"She doesn't like my pop-ups," Sammy mumbles, head down.

"Pua, is that what you said to Sammy?" I ask.

"No, not really," she replies. "I actually like his pop-ups, just not where I need to open my notebook."

"That lawnmower outside is so noisy, I couldn't hear Pua," Sammy states.

This is something I've noticed over and over in children diagnosed with ADD. It's not that they don't listen; it's that they listen too much. They listen to everything. I hadn't even noticed the lawnmower outside, but now that Sammy brings it up, I do notice that it's pretty noisy. I close the window. "Pua, tell Sammy again," I say.

Pua restates her assertion. This time Sammy says, "My pop-ups cover the table and Pua can't open her notebook."

"Sammy, do you have something to say to Pua?" I ask.

"I need my pop-ups. They're important to me. They remind me about colonial times."

"Pua, tell Sammy what you heard him say," I coach.

"You said that you need your pop-ups. But this is school. I need to do my schoolwork."

"Maybe I could put my pop-ups somewhere else," suggests Sammy "Like on this shelf, right behind me. Would that be better?"

Pua agrees. Sammy arranges several of his books and pop-ups on the shelf, and peace is restored, at least for the time being.

"What did you notice about Pua and Sammy's conversation?" I ask their tablemates, Halima and Robert.

"Sammy listened," said Halima.

"We could tell he was listening because he told Pua what he heard," adds Robert.

Later in the week I overhear Robert saying to Sammy, "Tell me what you heard me say." The students are learning some new skills.

Which behaviors should I let go of?
Which behaviors should I firmly stop?

I don't usually let students hop like a bunny through the circle or paw their classmates during lessons. But it's not always possible for teachers to address every issue in the moment. I recall my colleague, a fine teacher, who let Sammy read in a corner during lessons. By a few days into the school year, I empathize with that decision.

I'm caught between priorities and constraints. It's critical that all the students see, from the first hour of the first day of school, that their classroom is going to be a predictable and orderly place where everyone is safe, where everyone can learn. It's also true that it takes at least a week to develop our class rules and for me to introduce the "take a break" strategy and other ways of stopping misbehavior for those times when students forget or refuse to follow the rules. During this period, before we've established procedures for handling minor misbehaviors, it would be more disruptive to stop Sammy in the moment and "make" him sit still—probably an impossibility anyway.

Stuck between this particular rock and a hard place, I choose to ignore Sammy's less serious misbehaviors and stop the more harmful ones. For example, I let the hopping slide during those first few days. And Sammy's nuzzling of Frank is really only an "air nuzzle" without any physical contact. But when he actually thumps on Max, I stop him right away.

The Cuisenaire Rod incident, when Sammy threw the rods at me on the second morning of school, was one that I couldn't let slide. If the classroom is to be safe for everyone, it's crucial that hurting each other, either bodies or feelings, be out of bounds. It's also essential that the teacher's authority be a solid anchor to secure everyone in a safe harbor. Throwing things at anyone, especially the teacher, is unacceptable.

So what did I do? After swallowing hard and rapidly running through my limited options, I calmly called the office. The principal came immediately to get Sammy and called his mother.

This approach is in keeping with our schoolwide policy that any child who hits an adult or another child will be removed from the classroom, the family will be contacted, and the child will return to the class only after some type of conversation with the parent or guardian. This guideline is part of a comprehensive plan for helping children regain self-control.

When Sammy returned, he was penitent. He and I had a brief, private conversation in a quiet corner. We both knew he hadn't meant to throw the rods at me—he'd lost control. I accepted his apology and stated matter-of-factly that he needed to be kind to everyone's bodies and feelings so this classroom could be a safe place for all.

From my journal, September 7:

I'm thinking back to the flying Cuisenaire Rods. What could I have done to prevent that incident? I know that very bright children in general, and Sammy in particular, have strong ideas. They're compelled by an inner drive to explore and create in accord with their personal agendas. Would I have behaved differently if I'd thought ahead of time that Sammy might snatch the rods out of the bin? I probably would've asked the class, before passing out the rods, why they thought I was giving them only a few. I might've asked Sammy specifically for his ideas about this. I might've held the bin just slightly out of his reach as I passed out the rods. When I think about what might go wrong, I usually prepare a strategy. It's the behaviors that I haven't anticipated that cause disruption. The better I get to know Sammy, the more aware I'll be of what might go wrong. I can see that this will be my challenge, to anticipate those times when Sammy might erupt.

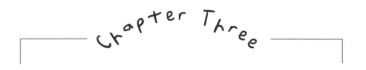

Tantrums, Writing Struggles, and the Beginnings of Self-Control

I t is only the fourth day of school when Sammy explodes again. The children are sharing their favorite books with the class and then putting the books into piles by category. It's a way for classmates to get to know each other as readers while learning about the concept of book genres.

Sofia has brought a collection of Native American myths to the circle and Manuel a Captain Underpants book. Sammy has brought an Eyewitness book with brief selections about Native American history, ideal for a history buff who has trouble paying attention.

Manuel tells the children why he likes the Captain Underpants series and sets his book carefully in the middle of the circle.

"Who has a book that might go with Manuel's?" I ask.

Zoe raises her hand. "My book is part of a series too, so it's like Manuel's." She places her Ramona book on top of the Captain Underpants book. I write "series books" on an index card and put the card on top of the stack. Children continue to share and place series books under the card.

The series books seem to be exhausted, so I ask, "Who has a book that might start a different category?"

Sofia tells about her Native American legends and places her book in the circle. "Could we call this category 'long ago'?" she asks.

"Does anyone else have a book that would fit in the 'long ago' category?" I ask. Paul has a novel set in Revolutionary War times, *Silver for General Washington*.

The students continue to share their books and create categories. At this stage it isn't important how the children categorize the books, as long as they're thinking about the idea of categories. Learning about the specific genres listed in the district language arts curriculum will come later.

Finally the center of the circle is full of stacks: funny books, long ago books, series books, fairy tales, bedtime stories, nonfiction books. Almost everyone's book is in a stack. Only Sammy is still clutching his.

"Where might you put your book?" I ask Sammy.

"I need a new stack, Eyewitness books about Native Americans," he replies.

Since the lesson is about categorizing, I decide to push Sammy on this one. "Sammy, there are a couple of categories that your book might fit in. What about 'long ago'?"

"All of the books in that stack are fiction. Mine is nonfiction."

"What about 'series books'? Yours is part of the Eyewitness series."

"But the series books are all fiction." Sammy's starting to dig in his heels.

"How about putting it in the nonfiction stack?" I ask. I'm feeling pressured for time. We have PE in less than ten minutes. I need to wrap up the lesson.

"Those books are all about science. Mine is about history," Sammy replies just a bit shrilly. He's responding to my tension.

The class is getting restless. My impatience mounts. "Sammy, make a choice. Nonfiction, series, or long ago."

"No! No! No!" Sammy screams. He lies on the floor, feet pounding, hands pummeling the rug. The lesson has dissolved without closure, the learning objectives lost in the chaos.

The rest of the class lines up for PE. Once they're in line, I try to calm Sammy.

From my journal, September 8:

Even after the Cuisenaire Rods, the literacy lesson was a surprise to me. Once again, I'm left feeling that if I had known what was coming next, I would have handled things differently. If I'd understood Sammy's potential to tantrum over a decision in a literacy lesson, I would have backed off and let him have his own category. Just because my plan called for categorizing books, doesn't mean all the children have to put their book in a category. And if I'd really thought it was important for Sammy to do it, I could have spoken with him briefly before the lesson.

If I just let him read in a corner, none of this would be happening. He'd be absorbed in a book. But the learning that we do as a group has value. Whether it's learning about possible uses of new materials or sharing a literacy lesson, Sammy has the potential to learn from whole-group lessons and to share his interesting ideas with peers. These experiences also help him be part of the group and feel the power of working with others.

A problem-solving conference: Establishing a private reminder signal to do what the teacher says

After the literacy lesson, it's clear that I need to take some further steps with Sammy, quickly. A one-on-one problem-solving conference seems in order.

For these conferences to go well, the teacher needs to identify one key issue to focus on. I think over these past four days. What's the one thing that most gets in the way of Sammy participating fully and calmly in school, and that will be productive to work on right now?

At first glance, it seems it's his lack of self-control. That's what leads to the tantrums and throwing things at me. But it'll be more effective to work on self-control slowly through strategies such as "take a break," which I'll be introducing to the class shortly.

I dig deeper for the root cause of Sammy's outbursts. They happen when he wants to decide about something and I've already made that decision for the good of the class. It's back to my authority as the teacher and leader of the classroom community. I need to clarify the basic classroom expectations of doing what the teacher says, and I need to ally with Sammy to show that I can help him with this challenge.

Having clarified that to myself, I invite Sammy to have lunch with me. "There are some things we need to talk over," I say.

"Yup," he says. He knows as well as I do that things aren't going so smoothly.

As the two of us sit down over lunch in the classroom, I begin by establishing what's going well. There's plenty to celebrate. "I've noticed that you love to read, especially when it helps you learn about history," I say.

"I love history," he replies and launches into another history joke. "Do you know where the Declaration of Independence was signed?"

I take the bait. "In Philadelphia?"

"Nope, at the bottom!" He chortles.

I laugh, too, and then, refocusing, I say, "Let's get back to the reason for this conference. In school it's important that kids do what the teacher says."

"I know that. When we said ideas for our classroom rules, I was the one who added 'listen to the teacher.'" It's uncanny the way children will often formulate a rule for the area of classroom life that they themselves have the most difficulty with.

"But I had such a good idea for something I could make with the Cuisenaire Rods," he continues, diving right in. "And I didn't want my book in a pile with anyone else's. My books aren't like the other kids'."

"I can see you feel that way," I say. "Nonetheless, in school, it's my job to teach the class. Sometimes that means I'll tell you to do something you don't want to do. We can figure out some way for you to show your ideas later that doesn't disrupt the group. But at that moment you need to do as I say."

Sammy looks serious and engaged. He does understand that kids are supposed to listen to the teacher. He just needs help following through.

"Would you like to work on this together?" I ask. "We could figure out a way to help you remember to listen and do what I say."

At this point, Sammy might say no. If he does, I would simply restate that it's important for him to follow my directions and look for other ways to address his behaviors. It's counterproductive to make children continue problem-solving with us if they're unwilling. Sammy, however, agrees to my offer.

"OK," he says, with a bit of skepticism in his voice. "It's just that I really wanted those rods. I really wanted my book in its own pile."

"So let's each suggest some ways that I could help you when you're about to say no to something I tell you to do," I say. My hypothesis is that if I can head off Sammy's behaviors in an early stage, they won't escalate into tantrums and open defiance. "One idea is that you could sit next to me during lessons, and I could put my hand on your shoulder when you start to argue, as a reminder." I jotted that idea down on a piece of paper.

"In second grade I had a chart. I got stars when I did the right thing," Sammy offers. I added his idea to the list without comment.

"You could bring sticky notes and a pencil to lessons, and when you start to get angry and feel that you might argue, you could write me a note," I add.

Sammy and I look at the list. "Which one do you think would work best for you?" I ask.

"How about if I sit next to you during lessons and you tap the floor to remind me if I start to argue?" he suggests.

"What if you also tap the floor if you notice that you're starting to get angry?" I say. "That way either of us might tap the floor. What do you think?"

Sammy agrees. I write down:

> *Sammy will listen to the teacher and do what she says. Ms. Crowe will remind him by tapping the floor if he starts to argue. Sammy will let Ms. Crowe know that he needs help by tapping the floor if he notices that he's getting angry.*

We both sign the paper. I put it in Sammy's file so that we can refer to it at subsequent conferences. It's time for recess, and Sammy heads out to the playground.

From my journal, September 10:

There's no question in my mind that Sammy and I will be meeting again. We accomplished a lot in our problem-solving conference though. Sammy knows I care about him, believe in him, and want him to succeed in school. There was a sense of teamwork in our conference. We now have a common understanding that his desire to express his unique ideas can take over and impel him into rocky territory. Sammy agreed to the goal of doing what the teacher says. And we came up with a plan, no matter how imperfect for now, to work together to help him behave more appropriately.

We teachers are constantly balancing the needs of the individuals in our class against the needs of the entire group. I want to meet Sammy's unique learning needs, and sometimes that will mean allowing him to follow his own path. On the other hand, I want to help Sammy learn to be part of a group, and sometimes that means he has to conform. Where is the balance with this particular child?

One thing I do know is that we need a way for Sammy to regain self-control when he starts to veer off. I'm relieved that tomorrow I'll be introducing "take a break" to the class.

RSC: the "Regain Self-Control" place

Our rules are posted on the wall, and we're trying them out to make sure they're just right. Now I can introduce "take a break," a strategy for stopping children's misbehavior when they forget the rules or choose not to follow them. By using "take a break" early, when the misbehavior is just beginning, we help students regain self-control when it's easiest to do so.

I'm confident that using "take a break" for minor losses of self-control will help Sammy. If he can use it as a positive tool to regain composure when he's just starting to get wound up, we should be able to avoid some major meltdowns like the kind we've had so far. But he and his classmates will only experience "take a break" as a helpful tool if I carefully introduce it as just that—a helpful tool.

The class sits in a circle. Sammy is right next to me. I'm using the strategy of proximity to help him attend to this social skills lesson.

I begin. "We've created our rules. We worked hard on them." Students nod. "But sometimes people break the rules. Sometimes we forget; sometimes we choose to break the rules. It's my job, as your teacher, to keep everyone safe, to help us all follow the rules."

I proceed to tell them about a time when it's hard for me to follow the rules, when I want to talk with my friends rather than listen during faculty meetings. Then I invite the students to share a time when it's hard for them to follow the rules. I'm trying to create a climate of empathy for the rule breaker.

Lori tells how she whispers to her friends when she's supposed to be reading. Jerry tells about how hard it is for him to sit and listen during lessons. Patricia says that she sometimes says mean things about other girls. Sammy shares that he says no to the teacher. The children are transfixed by this honest talk about rule breaking.

Once everyone has had a chance to share, I explain that in this class, when we begin to lose self-control, we're going to use a special place to pull ourselves together. "When I notice you misbehaving in small ways, I'll send you to our special place to regain self-control," I explain.

Next I model using "take a break." I model it before asking any student to model it so I can set a positive tone around its use and so I can demonstrate expected "take a break" behavior. "Pretend that I'm a student having trouble with an assignment, and I'm getting frustrated. The teacher sees that I'm about to do or say something unkind and tells me to go to our special place for regaining self-control." I quietly get up, go to the chair that I've set up, and take some deep breaths. "Now pretend the teacher has told me to come back." I happily return to the group.

I ask the students what they noticed. They have lots to say: I took deep breaths, I sat still in the chair, I walked quietly. Then several children get to practice walking calmly to the chair while the rest of us notice their behaviors.

Next I bring up a problem that often occurs as children are learning to use "take a break." "Sometimes I might send you to our special place to regain self-control, and you might not agree that you're starting to lose self-control," I say. "For example, I might send Jenny to our special place because I think she was whispering to Halima during a lesson, but she's only leaned over toward Halima. When that happens, you still need to go there. That's because at that moment the most important thing is to move quickly and quietly so the rest of the class can go on learning. Later on you can let me know that I made a mistake, but not then, while I'm teaching and the other students are learning."

Sammy says, "I'd like to show the class how not to act when the teacher tells you to regain self-control."

"Sammy," I reply, "in this class we show how to act. You may show the class how you *do* go to the special place." It's important that children act out only the positive behaviors, because if they act out the negative ones, those will likely be what they'll remember.

"But I can show saying no really well," Sammy insists.

Rather than argue, I simply tap the floor gently with my foot, using our signal.

Sammy sees my signal and nods. Nonetheless, he still wants to show defiance of teacher directions. He gets up and begins to get that characteristic look on his face when he starts to dig in his heels.

"We're only going to show the way we *do* go to the special place," I repeat firmly but calmly. Sammy acquiesces and demonstrates calm walking to the "take a break" chair. *It worked!* I silently exclaim to myself. *Heading off his problematic urges before they escalate seems to work!* I keep an objective outward appearance though. Publicly making a big deal of this would not be appropriate or effective.

The children name the chair the "RSC" for the "Regain Self-Control" place. Throughout this whole discussion, I've been careful not to use the word "time-out," as it can have such punitive connotations.

As the week continues, I make a point of sending a variety of children to the RSC—when they whisper to a friend during a group lesson or start to braid their neighbor's hair in the circle. I want them to understand that RSC is for small things, so that small things don't turn into bigger things.

Now I have another strategy that I can use with Sammy. I still tap my foot when I think he might be heading down a path toward frustration and defiance, but I also send him to the RSC. Sammy snatches Michele's book that she's brought to the circle for book share. "Sammy, RSC," I say. He goes peacefully and then returns in a few minutes. There's no question that Sammy uses the RSC place frequently, but most children go there sometimes, so it's not seen as "Sammy's chair."

From my journal, September 12:

We're off to a good start, Sammy and me. I like him and he knows that. That's the foundation. My colleagues were right, Sammy has lots of challenges. Paying attention to the lesson is a challenge, but we've had some success when I've encouraged him ahead of time and then have had him sit right next to me.

Partner work isn't going as well because it's not as closely supervised. In the short term, I need to keep him working with a variety of partners so no one child always has an inattentive partner. In the long term, I can teach him more effective collaboration skills.

Another big challenge is Sammy's tendency to lose control when he's been thwarted. It helps if I anticipate these moments and briefly talk to him ahead of time. It's also useful that he and I are building an alliance, complete with our tapping signal, to help him maintain control. The positive use of "take a break" for small things is shaping up to be an important tool as well.

Academic strengths and struggles

It's important to me that all students in this class succeed academically. I believe all children want to and can learn, but I also know that to learn at their best, many students need a teaching approach that's targeted to their individual learning style. Careful noticing of Sammy's successes and struggles will help me figure out an effective teaching approach for him.

Writing: "I hate to write. I don't want to have to write about history."

Today, week three of school, students are decorating their writers' notebooks, special journals in which they will write about their interests and passions.

We've been getting ready for these writers' notebooks since school started. The students have learned that we all have stories to tell. They've practiced storytelling by relaying family stories to each other. I've shared my writer's notebook and invited colleagues into our room to share their notebooks.

Now the children are invested in personalizing their notebooks. Some are putting stickers on the covers and are sharing these treasures with their tablemates. Others are drawing pictures of things they love and taping those to their covers.

Sammy has drawn a picture of George Washington, awkward and less evenly proportioned than classmates' drawings but recognizable by the wooden false teeth. Sammy struggles to use the scissors to cut out this portrait and then puts great globs of glue on the back of it. I'm reminded of his big wobbly letters. I make a mental note to work with him on small motor skills.

The next day, the children begin to list topics on the first page of their notebook. Titled "Things Close to My Heart" and written inside an outline of a heart, these are topics they might write about throughout the year.

I'm surprised to discover that Sammy is struggling to get an idea down on the paper. He has so many passions. What's this about?

"How about history, Sammy?" I ask.

"I hate to write," he declares. "I don't want to have to write about history."

I wonder if this is related to his difficulty with small motor skills. I'll watch and see what I can learn.

I offer Sammy the computer. "Do you want to create your heart-list on the computer?" I ask.

"Well, OK," he agrees. Five minutes later he's changing fonts, playing with the space bar and doesn't have a word on the screen yet. At my insistence he writes "History." He has a one-word list. I can see that there's a puzzle for me to pursue here.

Reading: Perfect comprehension scores

Sammy reads voraciously, mainly nonfiction. Surrounded by his wall of books, first he picks *The Smithsonian Book of Native Americans* and reads with absorption and comprehension. "Ms. Crowe, Ms. Crowe, did you know that people migrated from Siberia to our country more than 10,000 years ago?"

Required individual reading assessments are due in early October. I meet with Sammy individually, as I do with each of his classmates. He reads a nonfiction piece and then answers questions from me. His score is perfect, so I try a fiction piece from the next level up. Again, Sammy gets a perfect score.

We keep going, with a perfect score each time, until we reach the highest level at which we assess in third grade. He is a fluent reader with fine comprehension. I can see that part of my job this year will be to challenge Sammy as a reader.

Math: Complex thinking or jumbled ideas?

District-required math assessments have begun. Today the children have one math problem. They're to solve the problem using pictures, objects, and/or numbers, and they have to show their thinking using equations, diagrams, and words. This is not a new type of assignment. There have been similar expectations in earlier grades. Most children set to work drawing diagrams and writing about their thinking. They work alone, unusual for third grade so far. Up until now I've typically had them work together.

Sammy is happy to finally get to work by himself. He takes out a two-gallon bin of interlocking cubes and spreads them on the floor. He creates piles of various colors. I circulate around the room, checking in with children. When I get to Sammy, he says "Well, these are the buckets," but seems at a loss to explain how the "buckets" connect to the problem.

I announce that the forty-five minutes is up. Children turn in their papers. Sammy, frustrated, angrily strews the cubes around the room. "I didn't finish, I need more time, my buckets aren't full yet!" he shouts.

From my journal, September 24:

Did he have a plan? The "buckets" seem quite similar to the elaborate paper creation that he showed the class during our lesson on explaining your math thinking. Do these creations demonstrate some complex thinking, or are they unrelated to the math problem? Does he have a personal way of organizing his thoughts, or does he just need help with organization? Either could be true. I need to watch, ask the right questions, listen carefully.

Beginning an alliance with Sammy's family

No one knows Sammy better than his family. With their support, I can help Sammy have a year of learning and growth. Without it, the year might be something quite different. So it's crucial that I build an alliance with them.

Like most teachers', my year is punctuated by certain predictable communications with families. I had met Sammy's mother and brother at our meet-the-teacher event the day before school. I'd sent home a letter explaining classroom procedures and policies and asking for parents' perspectives on their child. After Sammy's Cuisenaire Rod incident I'd spoken briefly on the phone with his mother, explaining what had happened. I'd called her after the book sorting event to tell her that I was going to have a private problem-solving conference with Sammy.

I'd also called her a couple of times to tell her about something that went well: that he'd sat through the entire Morning Meeting or that he'd listened to Marie during their reading conference. Sammy's parents had attended our late September Back-to-School Night, at which I had explained the curriculum and taken questions.

But I had yet to have a private face-to-face conversation with any adult in Sammy's family. I call Sammy's mother and set up an appointment. I offer to meet with her before school, after school, or during one of my preparation periods. Mrs. Smith chooses a preparation period in the morning on Wednesday, her day off.

The children are at music class when Mrs. Smith arrives at the classroom door. I greet her warmly. We sit down together and I start talking about Sammy. First and foremost, I want her to know that I like him and that in many ways he is doing well in third grade. "Sammy arrives every morning with a big smile on his face," I say. "He often has a joke to tell me or a fact to share."

"He is a funny kid, isn't he?" she replies with a little laugh.

Next, I raise the issues. We don't have a lot of time as the children's music class will end in twenty minutes. "We're working on sitting in the circle for lessons. He's really trying. We've developed some strategies to help him."

"Sammy's told me about the floor tapping," Mrs. Smith says, "and about the RSC chair. He likes to have a place to go when he starts to get upset."

I smile. "I want it to be a safe place, a helpful tool for all of us."

Most of all, I want to know if Sammy has similar incidents at home and, if so, how Mrs. Smith handles them. "So," I ask, "is Sammy ever defiant at home? Does he ever get out of control?"

"Oh, yeah," she says. "He can have quite a temper."

"What do you do when that happens?"

"Well, I try to plan ahead. He doesn't like changes. If he's watching TV, he doesn't want to get up. It helps if I warn him ahead of time, like telling him we're having dinner in five minutes."

So I haven't really thought about Sammy and transitions. Since it's so early in the year, I'm giving the whole class lots of pre-alerts before transitions, but later I'll be expecting them to handle transitions more independently. At that point I'll need to pay careful attention to how Sammy manages these moments. Perhaps a private encouraging word beforehand will help, as it seems to help before challenging situations in general.

Mrs. Smith has some questions, too. "How're things going with friends?" she asks. "He's not a big baseball or football player, and I know the other boys are into that. Do they play with him?"

"There is a small group of boys who chase each other around the playground at recess. He runs around with them," I answer honestly. "They're not quite playing together, and yet they're happy to be close to each other," I elaborate.

"Working with classmates is hard for him," I continue. I try to be as concrete as possible. "He can annoy classmates with his pop-ups and the way he touches kids, but we're working on it."

"He told me about the pop-ups conference his table had," she replies. "I tell him, 'Just don't make those pop-ups,' but it doesn't help." I can imagine she's been hearing about Sammy's creations overtaking the classroom for a few years now.

It's time for me to pick up the class. I thank Mrs. Smith for coming and walk her out of the building on my way to the music room. As we walk downstairs, she brings up the fact that Sammy's younger than the rest of the class. "When he started school, we thought that since he's so bright he'd do well in kindergarten even though he was only four."

As I walked down the last flight to the music room, I mused on Mrs. Smith's concerns about Sammy's friendships. He's younger than most, less athletic, and has interests that others don't share. My experience is that children can be accepting of great differences when the teacher provides an example of acceptance for all. My challenges this year will include teaching Sammy the social skills that will help him make friends and teaching his classmates that in our room there's a place for everyone.

PART 2

SETTLING IN

October through December

Chapter Four

Coaching for Success

We've been in school for nearly two months now and no longer feel like a group of strangers. After many getting-to-know-you activities in Morning Meeting, we all know that Garret loves to fish and Sofia enjoys drama. We know that Frankie is part of a large blended family while Michele's family consists of herself and her mom.

We're building awareness of each other's learning styles, too. We know that Halima can be quiet, fading into the background listening to the teacher. Jenny, on the other hand, lets her ideas bubble out without hesitation. Knowing each other builds empathy, even across the lines of culture, race, gender, and personal style.

Students in this class know that they're expected to listen to and respect everyone. I've taught how to listen and how to respond both honestly and kindly to classmates' ideas. The children have practiced these behaviors, agreeing about what they look like and sound like.

I think it's time to plan a party together, to celebrate being together for two months. A class meeting to plan a party will give everyone a chance to pull together all their newfound skills and their knowledge of each other to create something everyone will enjoy. I decide to call it our "Fall Fun" party.

Coaching Sammy for a successful class meeting

I now know Sammy well enough to know that I have to prepare him for our upcoming party planning. Once Sammy has an idea, it's hard for him to let go of it. This could be a problem in group decision making, and to have our first class meeting marked by one of Sammy's meltdowns would be especially damaging to the class's sense of competence. Sure, I'll be reminding all the students to listen to each other's ideas with an open mind. But it doesn't do any good to remind someone of a skill that he doesn't yet have. Sammy will need some specific teaching about being open to classmates' ideas.

While at the reading table with Sammy finishing up a running reading record, I raise the issue. "Sammy, this afternoon we're going to have a class meeting to plan our Fall Fun party."

He looks excited. "Maybe we could have a history party!"

"Do you think other kids would enjoy a history party?" I ask.

"Well, we could have history jokes."

"Sammy," I say in a friendly but firm tone, "kids might like a history party, but my guess is that most of them would prefer to play fun fall games."

"Maybe we could have a history party later in the year?" he bargains.

"Maybe," I agree. "It's fine if you bring up the idea of a history party in our class meeting. But it's also important that you listen to your classmates' ideas respectfully as well as sharing your own. Which of our classroom rules will help you remember to do that?"

Sammy looks up at the poster of classroom rules that we had all worked hard to create.

"Respect and care for everyone?" he asks.

"I think that covers listening respectfully to others' ideas." I add, "It's also important that you actually consider their ideas. I know you want more friends. People will feel friendly toward you if you're friendly to them, and that includes considering their ideas."

I'm trying to make it real. Kids do get irritated when someone doesn't think about their ideas. Right now they're all making an effort to follow our classroom rules and be respectful and caring. Sammy's thoughtful response to their ideas can keep that momentum going.

"Let's practice," I say. "I'm going to pretend to share an idea. You're going to keep a friendly face and think about my idea. What might that friendly face look like?"

Sammy smiles and nods his head.

"OK," I say. "I'd like to bob for apples at our party."

Sammy starts to make an angry face. I tap my foot. His lips turn up into just a suggestion of a smile, and he nods. He might even be considering my idea.

"So when you thought about my idea, what was going on for you?" I ask.

"I was thinking about what it would be like to put my face in that cold water. I don't like bobbing for apples."

"So you considered my idea, kept a friendly face, and thought about how you'd feel bobbing for apples. You didn't agree with me, but you were respectful." I'm careful to let Sammy know that I'm not asking him to pretend agreement but rather to listen respectfully. I want students to own their opinions.

"That's your goal in the class meeting: to keep a friendly face and listen and consider your classmates' ideas respectfully," I summarize. "Do you think you're ready?"

"Yup!" Sammy says. He's willing to try something that might help him develop some real friendships, friendships in which someone would actually seek him out to play.

The Fall Fun party-planning meeting

The children are gathered in a circle. Sammy's right next to me. As the last students finish their cleanup from the previous activity and join us in the circle, I whisper privately to Sammy, "Remember, consider others' ideas." He smiles and responds, "And keep a friendly face." We're ready to go!

"Today is an important day," I tell the children. "We're going to have our first class meeting. We'll have many class meetings this year. Sometimes we'll meet to solve problems that affect all of us. Today we're going to meet to plan an event, a Fall Fun party for next Friday." The children are excited.

"We're going to decide together what we'll do at the party," I say. "But first, which of our rules might help us do this in a way that feels fair to everyone?"

The children look up at the rules. Lori raises her hand and offers, "Respect and care for everyone?"

"How might that rule help us?" I ask.

Sammy raises his hand. "If we respect each other, we'll consider each other's opinions." He's thinking about our earlier discussion.

"Yes," I say. "That will help us plan a party that will be fun for everyone."

Patricia chimes in, "How about 'listen'? We'll need to listen to each other's ideas." I nod.

"OK, thumbs up if you're ready to follow our rules," I say. Deciding what to do at a party can raise emotions that might cause children to forget the rules. This physical step of affirming by showing thumbs serves as an extra reminder to the students and lets me know that everyone's in agreement. I look around. Everyone's thumb is up.

"First we'll go around the circle," I explain. "You each may contribute an idea for a game to play at our party. If you don't have an idea, just say 'pass.'"

To encourage children to think creatively, it's important to start by having them freely brainstorm without evaluating how fun or practical any idea is, saving that evaluation as a next step. So I add, "We're just getting ideas out right now. We won't comment on people's ideas, but just contribute new ideas. I'll record."

We go around the circle. Manuel suggests playing Four Corners. Sofia suggests Thumbs Up. Zoe suggests bobbing for apples. Sammy starts to make a disgusted face. I gently tap the floor and his face smoothly glides into a neutral expression. Jenny mentions eating doughnuts off a string. Sammy would like to make fall pop-ups. He's actually modified his wishes since our conference and is suggesting something his classmates might choose to do.

"Next, each of us will make a comment, if we'd like, about why we like a particular idea or why we think an idea might not work. We really need to pay attention to our rule to respect and care for everyone now," I say. I feel confident having the children do this step because by now they know a lot about each other, which helps them see things from each other's perspective. And, we've had plenty of practice in giving each other honest yet kind feedback—for example, on each other's ideas about a book or on each other's writing—so they have experience using the appropriate words, tone, and facial expression.

As we go around the circle this second time, Garret tells about how much fun it was at his birthday party when people ate doughnuts off a string. Paul mentions he doesn't like the idea of putting your face in water to bob for apples because other kids have put their faces in there, too. Sammy nods vigorously at that statement. Zoe, the one who suggested bobbing for apples, says maybe each student could have their own bucket of water.

When it's my turn, I point out that two kinds of activities have been proposed: whole-group ones (like Four Corners) and small-group ones that everyone can cycle through (like eating doughnuts off a string). We're only going to have time for one kind, I explain.

Max says we play whole-group games a lot as energizer breaks throughout the day but we've never gotten to play small-group games like doughnuts on a string. Many students smile and nod at this comment.

I wonder if a consensus is emerging and decide to give it a try. "Let's see where we are as a group right now. Put your thumb up if you'd prefer that we play a number of small-group activities, with everyone rotating through."

Every thumb goes up. It's almost dismissal time, and I decide that this is a positive note on which to end our first class meeting. "Tomorrow we'll collect more ideas for small-group games as part of the morning message. Then we'll pick which ones to play," I say. "I want to congratulate everyone on working so well as a community during our first class meeting. You followed our rules and reached an agreement."

As the children pack up to go home, I whisper to Sammy, "You did it. You were respectful and considered others' ideas."

Attempts in "the friends department"

In the classroom, Sammy is a loner, engaged with his own passions, surrounded by his stacks of history books and his pop-ups of scenes from history. But he also approaches other children, wanting interaction. He seldom
pokes and paws them these days, a result of my specific social skills teaching
and the consistent use of the RSC. Too often, however, his way is to tell
other children what to do. "I made a Valley Forge pop-up. Now you make
the river to go with it." Children often walk away from this lack of mutuality.
Clearly, Sammy needs help in "the friends department," as he calls it.

I observe. It's time for the students to invite classmates to be their lunch
partners. This is something they do regularly, a practice to build an inclusive
community. I pick Popsicle® sticks from a jar to determine who gets to ask
first, second, and so on. As he does each time it's his turn, Sammy asks Max.
Max is unfailingly polite and eats with Sammy, but his face doesn't beam
with delight when asked. Even more telling, Max doesn't invite Sammy
when it's his turn to do the asking.

Sammy misses the subtle fact that other children ask a variety of partners. He can be intense, and I have a feeling that Max—and other children
as well—will enjoy being with him more if they're not with him so much.

At recess Sammy races around the playground, chasing other children
but without a lot of interaction. It's a sort of parallel play tag game that

doesn't require an "it," boundaries, or rules. Garret races with them. So does Paul. Either of them could be a potential friend for Sammy. I'll suggest Sammy invite them on some lunch partner days.

Getting on Sammy's side

Sammy has many good days, but there are also plenty of bad ones. He digs in his heels and refuses to write his science journal entry. He crawls behind the bookcase when it's time to write math journal entries and keeps sticking his head out and making faces at Max. He rolls on the floor during handwriting practice. On days like that, by the time the children leave for the day, I have a headache.

Half an hour of writing and reflecting in my journal usually helps dissipate my annoyance with Sammy's behaviors. I need to make sure that as the year goes on, I deepen my relationship with Sammy rather than pull away because of feeling more annoyed with him. Taking time to reflect is crucial for this relationship deepening. I think about students on my way home. I talk over the day with a trusted colleague while we take an after-school walk. These moments all help build my understanding of the children and my feelings of friendly acceptance toward them.

Today, Sammy once again asks Max to be his lunch partner. Annoyance flickers across Max's face as Sammy happily shouts, "Max, Max, I want to eat with you today!" Max is getting a little less patient with Sammy.

I decide to act. It's my recess duty day, and I approach Sammy on the playground. "Would you like to sit on the bench and have a private chat for a few minutes? There's something I'd like to discuss with you." This discussion is a choice. If he'd rather play, I'd find another time to talk with him. He does, however, want to talk. I'm not surprised. Sammy likes to chat with adults.

Sammy and I sit together, privately, on the bench. "Sammy," I say, "I've noticed that every time it's your turn to invite a lunch partner, you invite Max."

"Yup," he says, "I like Max a lot. I think I'm making progress with him. He's getting to like me more." So Sammy understands that Max doesn't seek him out and isn't thrilled to spend time with him.

I try to put myself in Sammy's shoes. He so wants Max to like him. "Sammy," I say sympathetically, "I think you'll make more progress with Max if you don't ask him to eat with you every time you get the Popsicle stick. Kids like to eat with different friends. Max is going to get irritated with you if you ask him every time."

"But I am making progress with him, I know I am," Sammy insists. There's that characteristic rigidity when I try to redirect him. He is persistent.

"Did you notice the way he rolled his eyes a little bit when you asked him today?" I ask. "You and Max could be friends, Sammy. You like to do many of the same things. I think he likes you now, but he's not going to continue to like you unless you give him some space. There are other kids who would like to be your partner. You could ask Garrett or Paul."

Sammy must have noticed the hint of eye rolling as well because he says, "OK, next time I'll ask someone else."

The next time I draw Sammy's stick, I look at him meaningfully. He says, "Garret, will you eat lunch with me today?" Garret grins and says, "Sure." Only yesterday, during lunch invitations, Garret had said, "I wish someone would invite me for a change."

Events like this one reinforce Sammy's growing understanding that I'm on his side. I give him advice that actually helps. Garret is happy to have lunch with Sammy, and Max is more tolerant the next time Sammy asks because he had a break. I make sure Sammy knows I'm on his side by being on his side.

My role as everyone's teacher

I can't allow all of my attention to go to Sammy, though. There are twenty-five students in this class. Marie has a diagnosis of autism. Paul has difficulty remembering things and is afraid to take a risk. Pua pretends to read books beyond her level at reading time and scrawls non sequiturs in her journal at writing time. How can I meet all of their needs?

My most important goal is to establish a community where everyone is included, an atmosphere of safety and trust. Paul needs to feel that we all accept him the way he is, that it's safe to participate in a multiplication game even if he may not remember the math facts. Pua needs to feel OK reading books that she can read even if they aren't "third grade books." It's paramount that I model accepting behavior, guide the class in practicing these behaviors, and hold them accountable for being accepting and respectful.

And it's vital that the children who are doing just fine get my attention, too. My job is to notice everyone. I need to make sure Sofia has a turn to answer during math, even though she tends to fade into the background. It's important that we hear from the quiet as well as the outspoken children.

I prep Paul for a math game ahead of time. "We're reviewing subtraction facts today," I say to him. "Which one are you really sure of?"

"Fourteen minus seven equals seven?" he asks uncertainly.

"OK," I say, "I'll make sure to call on you for that one." I turn over cards. When I come to fourteen minus seven, I say, "Paul?" and he answers confidently, "Seven."

Meanwhile, Sammy is sticking therapy putty on his nose and letting it dribble down into his mouth. Without missing a beat, I reach over and, with a tissue, remove the putty from his nose.

I look over at Sofia. I know she knows these math facts though she's not raising her hand to give the answers. When I flip over the next card, I invite her to answer. She does so, quietly and correctly.

After the lesson, as we transition to reading, I quietly speak to Paul. "I could see you're learning your subtraction facts." Then I speak to Sammy. "I'll keep the putty until tomorrow. Then we'll try again." And I say to Sofia, "I can see you practiced your math facts."

It's all about keeping the momentum of the lesson going so that everyone can learn. Quiet reinforcements and redirections during lessons need to be seamless so they don't interrupt that momentum. More in-depth conversations about additional supervision or structures that I'll be providing to stop negative behaviors can take place after the lesson is over.

When Sammy acts out, it benefits the whole class if I remain calm and positive. I know that the students are more likely to feel calm and secure if I'm feeling that way myself. They reflect my moods and behavior. Admittedly, that takes some self-control on my part, and sometimes I feel like visiting the RSC chair myself.

Days of Peaceful Learning, Days of Turmoil

Things are calming down a bit with Sammy. There are more days of peaceful learning and fewer days of turmoil. Guiding him proactively—using reminders, reinforcements, and redirections as consistently as possible—has been crucial in bringing about this small but significant improvement.

As his mother suggested, I'm giving Sammy plenty of warnings before transitions so he'll be ready to shift gears when it's time. "Sammy," I whisper, "five minutes until the end of readers' workshop." A couple of minutes later I say, "Stop reading when you get to the end of the chapter" and watch to make sure he does. When it's time to move on to math, he puts his book away.

I'm using "take a break" consistently to stop misbehaviors early, for Sammy and all the students. Sammy's frequent trips to the RSC chair are keeping his small moments of disequilibrium from turning into major meltdowns. The RSC is adding a measure of peace to the whole classroom.

I'm using that powerful tool, positive and specific reinforcing language, to let Sammy know when he's being successful. "I noticed that you went to RSC, took a few breaths, and regained self-control without a reminder from me," I softly comment. Sammy appreciates that I speak to him privately so he doesn't get embarrassed by loud announcements about his behavior, whether it's on- or off-target behavior.

I'm also using specific reminders for all children when they just start to get off track. Reminders work well with Sammy, especially when they're prompt and firm. "Sammy, remember our agreement. Pop-ups in your locker during math," I say as he starts to create yet another scene from history during math. If I remind him before he's fully engaged with his creation, he'll put it away without a tantrum.

If he's already engaged in an off-task activity, I give a clear, firm redirection. "Sammy, pop-up away or it'll be in my closet." If I use redirecting language quickly enough, it's effective.

Helping Sammy listen in the group continues to be a daily requirement, but he is improving. I remind him before we begin a lesson and have him sit near me so that my presence is a continuous reminder. When he shows that he's being attentive, I quietly whisper reinforcements. "You responded to Juan's contribution that time. I could tell you were paying attention to Juan's ideas."

Chattering commentary during whole-class lessons

For sure, there are things about Sammy that continue to be a puzzle. The class is sitting in a circle, ready to begin a lesson about writing responses to literature. The focus is on supporting one's ideas with specific details. Sammy is next to me, and I've given him a brief, private reminder about listening. Introducing the topic to the group, I say, "This one might seem hard at first, but I know you'll be able to do it." Sammy joins in as a little echo, "Yup, hard as winter at Valley Forge."

I start to wonder, "How often does Sammy do this? Does echoing me help Sammy attend?" Lots of seven-year-olds subvocalize or whisper to themselves as they read. Maybe Sammy subvocalizes, more loudly than some, during group discussions. I start to pay more attention to his mutterings.

When we discuss our Monarch butterflies in their chrysalis, he comments, "Cozy as my bed at home." As we discuss bus behavior before a field trip, he mutters about kids who bother him on the school bus in the morning. His mental tape is playing for all of us to hear.

From my journal, November 1:

How much of Sammy's chattering through lessons is part of his learning style? How much of it is developmental? If it's helping him attend, which it seems to be doing since it's usually about the topic at hand, I don't want to stop it altogether. But I want to help him modify behaviors that are distracting other children. They aren't complaining now, but his running commentary is pretty loud and could become irritating to them over time. I think I'll work with him on turning down the volume. That's what I would do with a seven-year-old who whispers along as she reads.

"No! No! No! I'm not going! I don't want to go!"

Although I'm using reminders and redirections a lot, I don't always calibrate them with pinpoint accuracy. We're getting ready for our second field trip to the nature center. Children are hurrying to get the attendance and lunch count in to the office before we leave for the morning. Parent chaperones are in the classroom, ready to go. I'm supervising last-minute bathroom trips and reorganizing each parent's list of children to supervise, since one chaperone didn't show up and three children are unexpectedly out sick. There's an unusual level of chaos for our classroom. Sammy slips off to a corner and starts to create pop-ups. I don't notice his absence until the children are in line with their coats on and I'm taking last-minute roll.

"Sammy?" I ask. "Sammy?" No answer.

Then Zoe points out, "He's over there in the corner by the art area." Sure enough, there he is, surrounded by scraps of colored paper, busily cutting out an elaborate Wampanoag fishing weir.

"Sammy, it's time to go," I say calmly. "You can clean up when we get back."

"Just a minute," he responds. "I have to finish weaving my weir."

"Sammy, it's time to leave now." I'm still calm, but my voice is firm and authoritative. Sammy keeps cutting.

Twenty children and five adult chaperones watch as I walk over to Sammy, take the scissors out of his hand, and say, "Sammy. The bus is waiting. Get in line now."

"No! No! No!" he shrieks. "I'm not going! I don't want to go!"

I'm outwardly calm but my internal tension is mounting. Sammy and I are on display. I take a deep breath and quickly think through my options. Leave him at school with an administrator? That would be my last resort, as the trip is a learning event, part of our curriculum. Get help from the school counselor or an administrator? It's going to take a while to round up adult assistance, and the busses are waiting. I decide to make use of what I have, the parent chaperones. Leaving Sammy, I give the parents their group lists and ask them to walk their groups down to the bus.

With the audience gone and the room quiet, both Sammy and I relax just a bit. I calmly pick up Sammy's pop-up and put it in the closet. I get out his coat and tell him, "We'll discuss this when we get back from the trip. Now it's time to go." Bringing him a drink of water, I say, "The other kids are waiting for you on the bus. Remember, Max is your seat partner." Sammy perks up a bit at the prospect of sitting with the coveted Max. We start down the hall together. By the time we're on the bus, he's happy to be headed to the nature center.

From my journal, November 7:

The issue is a recurring one. Sammy's internal rhythms impel him forward—the pop-up must be completed—but they conflict with the needs of the group. In a different world, I can easily imagine Sammy spending his day with one tutor who follows his impulses, mining them for learning opportunities. Yet there is much for Sammy to learn when he matches his rhythms to the group. The world is made up of people working together, and no matter how creative Sammy's ideas are, they can be enhanced by his learning to collaborate.

Part of my job is to teach Sammy how to move with the group. I teach him with pre-alerts and specific coaching. I can strengthen this teaching by adding other strategies for stopping misbehavior besides "take a break." Tomorrow I'll tell him that the art corner is closed to him for two days. Even though he benefits from the small-motor practice, it's more important right now to remove the objects related to his misbehavior.

The next morning I have a brief, private conversation with Sammy as the children arrive. "Remember when we talked about how important it is for kids to do what the teacher tells them?" I remind Sammy.

"Yup," he answers. "I know it's important. But yesterday I forgot."

"Because you wouldn't stop weaving your weir yesterday even when I told you that it was time to get on the bus, I'm going to close the art supplies to you for today and tomorrow. You can use the scissors and colored paper again on Monday." I deliver this news with a neutral tone of voice. My calm, matter-of-fact stance helps Sammy to feel matter-of-fact about it as well.

Sammy, in his calm state a day after the incident, knows that being separated from the art supplies for two days is reasonable.

"OK," he says and heads off to answer the morning message.

Academic revelations, breakthroughs, struggles

Math: Aces the problem-solving,
flounders in "explain your thinking"

We're all at the computer lab for a required computerized math assessment. Based on all math skills that will be taught in third grade, the assessment contains many questions that are beyond the children's current skills. It's meant to gather baseline information to guide teaching, and the children are not expected to be able to answer all the questions.

Most children wiggle and whine, frustrated that there are so many questions they don't understand. Garret soldiers through, randomly picking answers. Sammy puts the earphones on, drowns out all outside stimulus, and begins to work.

Looking over his shoulder, I realize that Sammy's getting every question right, even the "problem-solving" questions. At the end of the period, the rest of the class, relieved that such a stressful event is over, races out to recess. Sammy, however, is downright disappointed. Later in the day, he begs me to let him finish the math assessment. I pull his assessment up on the classroom computer. He puts on the earphones and happily finishes.

After school I look at his score: 100% with the exception of the spots where he had to write to explain his thinking.

From my journal, November 10:

So, Sammy knows every math skill taught in third grade. He can see the solutions to challenging problems but has difficulty explaining his thinking. As his teacher, my job is to help him learn to do this explaining. Also, he can work with absorption when outside stimulus is blocked, as it was with the earphones. I wonder if there are ways that I can offer him that lack of distraction in the classroom.

"Charles is three times the age of his sister, Sophie," I say to the class. "In two years he'll be twice Sophie's age. How old are Charles and Sophie now?" Bubbling over with excitement, Sammy raises his hand right away. "Charles is six and Sophie is two," he announces proudly.

When presented with a problem-solving challenge, Sammy announces the answer in a flash. Yet we keep coming back to the issue of explaining his thinking in equations, diagrams, and words. He gets out the manipulatives and makes piles all over the rug. By the end of the period, the manipulatives are a jumble and Sammy is hiding under the nearest table.

I sit down with Sammy during a problem-solving challenge. "Sammy,"
I say, "would you like some help?"

"Well … ," he replies, "I got out the cubes. They're going to help me.
Pretty soon I'll be ready."

"When I was in high school," I say, "my algebra teacher taught us how
to be efficient in our solutions. Let's see if you and I can figure out an efficient way to solve this problem. I'll bet you won't even need these cubes." I
encourage students who might benefit from concrete support to use manipulatives. Sammy, however, is easily solving challenging problems in his head.
I think the manipulatives are just adding an unnecessary layer.

First I read the problem aloud to Sammy: "Marla's family is collecting
maple sap to fill a small evaporator. The evaporator holds 30 gallons and they
need to fill it up. They have buckets that hold 5 gallons, 3 gallons, 4 gallons,
and 6 gallons. If Marla works with her brother and sister, each with a different size bucket, how many bucketfuls will it take to fill the evaporator?"

"Hmmm," says Sammy, "I think it'll work if they use the 4, 6, and 5
gallon."

"How do you know that?" I ask.

"I just know it," he says.

"Let's try to show your thinking by making a table," I continue. I take
a piece of lined paper and draw three columns on it. I label them—bucket

size, number of buckets, total gallons. Under bucket size I label three lines—4 gallon, 6 gallon, 5 gallon. "Now, what should I do next?" I ask Sammy.

"Five plus five equals ten," he says, "so put two buckets on the 5 gallon line." I surmise that he's thinking about thirty as a multiple of ten but isn't quite ready to express it that way yet. "Then put '10' in the 'total' column."

"How many more gallons do you need?" I ask.

"I need another twenty, and four plus six equals ten, so put two buckets of 4 gallons and two buckets of 6 gallons."

I fill in the columns, with two buckets of 4 and two buckets of 6. We add up the totals column: $8 + 12 + 10 = 30$ gallons. Later, as children share their solutions with the class, Sammy proudly displays his efficient chart.

Writing: The blank "Dear Nick" letter

We're studying cursive. During handwriting lessons, Sammy forms his newly learned cursive letters slowly but precisely, using the midline on the paper to keep the letters proportionally sized. Like many children who have difficulty controlling their manuscript letters, Sammy is benefiting from this fresh start of learning a new handwriting system now that he has more mature small-muscle control.

Sammy loves to practice cursive. Nonetheless, being able to form letters correctly isn't helping him compose his ideas in writing. Whatever the writing assignment, Sammy's paper is immediately recognizable by its large blank spaces. He's so articulate when sharing ideas in the give-and-take of personal conversation or classroom discussion, but when asked to talk about something that he knows he'll be expected to write about, he freezes up. Cursive writing has provided a confidence boost for Sammy, but it's not the solution to his reluctance to write.

It's Friday morning and the children are writing their weekly letters home to their families about their week in school. Based on what I observed during the computerized math assessment, I've offered Sammy the use of the computer to write his letter. I ask him who he's going to write to, and he says, "My brother Nick." At my suggestion, he puts on the earphones to block out classroom noise.

I circulate around the room, supporting students as they compose their sentences, check their spelling, and make sure their letters are just right. I circle back to see how Sammy is doing. He has "Dear Nick" on his computer screen and is busily changing the font.

"What's going on?" I ask him, genuinely interested in why he hasn't written after fifteen minutes on his own.

"I don't have anything to say." Sammy, with his constant subvocalizing, always seems to have something to say.

"Did you look at our chart?" I ask, reminding him of the chart that the class created, listing the many events of the past four days.

"Nothing on that chart is exciting. Nick knows about all of those things. He was already in third grade."

"I'll bet he'd like to read about what you're doing," I coax. "And you can tell him how you feel about those events. What about our trip to the nature center? You found a salamander under a log."

"Salamanders aren't so special. I wish I'd found an arrowhead." Irritation creeps into Sammy's voice.

I'm mindful that I need to check on other students. I need to read all their finished letters before they go home. I'm feeling that pressure and don't have time to stand here negotiating with Sammy. Also, I suspect this negotiation could go on and on.

"Sammy," I say, with more than a little irritation in my voice, "you need to write at least two sentences. I'll be back in five minutes to check on your progress."

From my journal, November 14:

Sammy never did finish his letter today. "Dear Nick" was his maximum output, and when I printed that out, he balled it up and threw it away. He was able to do math problems with absorption when sitting at the computer with earphones on. But, under the same conditions, picking a topic from the class-brainstormed list and writing a few sentences was insurmountable.

I'm guessing that Sammy's difficulty today with his letter home relates to his difficulty with writing about his math thinking. In both cases, there is understanding and even an assigned topic, but composition is daunting. Writing is tough for many children. It involves using so many skills simultaneously: calling up your ideas, putting them in logical order, turning them into sentences, writing those sentences on paper, all the while remembering letter formation, spelling, punctuation, and capitalization. I don't know what's making writing so hard for Sammy in particular. It could be any of a variety of causes or combination of causes, from a power struggle stemming from deep lack of confidence in this area to true language processing difficulties, with many other possibilities in between. For now I'm gathering information, trying strategies, hoping to build on strengths and successes.

I learn from November conferences

November parent–teacher conferences are a staple of school life. By November I've actually had sit-down, face-to-face conferences with many of the students' families. I've spoken with many on the phone to report good news or to discuss a puzzle about some aspect of their child's well being. I've sent home frequent written communications.

Nonetheless, a formal conference week offers an opportunity to gather information, to assess and perhaps change direction in my work with a student. For this reason, I begin by having students prepare a portfolio of work samples that show their progress in reading, writing, and math. I then meet privately with each student. The student shares her samples with me and talks about how she feels things are going academically and socially. I often learn things that I didn't know in the course of these student-teacher conferences.

When I meet with Sammy and ask how things are going with friends, his response is unchanged from earlier conversations: "I think I'm making progress with Max."

When I ask Max the same question in his private conversation with me, he says, "I like playing with Juan, Paul, Chris, Alex, Garret, Manuel, Jerry, Frankie, and Robert."

"What about Sammy?" I ask.

"I want to be respectful and friendly to Sammy, but I'd like it better if he didn't keep asking me to be his lunch partner over and over," Max replies.

So there it is, in a nutshell. Max wants to treat everyone respectfully but he wants to play with almost any other boy except Sammy.

"Sammy doesn't talk with me. He just tells me about history over and over," Max continues. So Sammy could benefit from some specific conversational skills.

The irony here is that I can see why Sammy is drawn to Max. They actually have a lot in common. They're the two youngest students in our class, both still seven in November. They each have a great sense of humor. They're fun and funny. If Sammy could back off a bit, they might become true friends.

When I meet with Garret, he tells me that he likes to play with Marie and Sofia, and he wishes he had more friends. I remember how pleased Garret was when Sammy invited him to lunch. "Why don't you ask Sammy to be your lunch partner sometime?" I ask.

"I wish he'd ask me," Garret replies. "I don't want to always be the one doing the asking." I point out to Garret that Sammy has invited him once, but he still hasn't invited Sammy.

After these student-teacher conferences, I meet privately with their parents. (I wait until the spring to hold three-way parent-student-teacher conferences.) Again, I learn so much.

Sammy's mom is highly focused on Sammy's social life. "The other kids don't call him. My older son gets lots of calls from his friends."

Max's mom reports that Max complains about the way Sammy "follows him around." "I'm happy that Max is in a classroom where he's expected to be respectful and friendly to everyone," she says. "But can't Sammy sometimes eat lunch with a different student?"

From my journal, November 21:

I can see that I need to take more action here. Sammy is so single minded in his concerns and attachments that he won't allow Max the space he needs unless I explicitly tell him to. Tomorrow I'm going to tell Sammy that he can invite Max to eat lunch with him only once every two weeks. Other kids—Garret. for example ---will be happy to eat with Sammy.

[...] g that Sammy just tells him about his-

[...] up before. I need to give Sammy a lit-

[...] versation. I suspect other kids could

[...] ble-class role-play on this.

[...] lunchtime conversation

[...] d that many of you have been ask-

[...] ith you." The children smile and

[...] to everyone. "Sometimes, though,

[...] don't know very well yet, you

[...] g to talk about that both of you

[...] n lunchtime conversation, but we

[...] e that I'm raising today.

[...] igure out what you and your lunch partner have in common that you might both enjoy talking about?"

We go around the circle. Garret says, "You could ask your partner what kind of music he likes."

"You could ask what they like to do after school," adds Pua.

"You could think about what your partner has shared at share time in Morning Meeting," says Patricia.

I write the children's ideas on chart paper. "We're going to put on a play using one of these ideas," I say. "I'll go first. Sammy, would you like to be my partner?"

I pick Sammy because I want him to have practice with this skill. I'm going to take the lead role first. I believe Sammy will be successful in the secondary role. Sammy agrees to be in this little play, so I say to the class, "I'm going to pick one of these ideas to see if I can figure out something that Sammy and I would both be interested in talking about. I'm going to try thinking about something that Sammy shared during Morning Meeting."

"Hmm," I think aloud for the benefit of the class. "Sammy shared that he likes Penguin Club on the Internet, but I've never been on Penguin Club. He's shared that he likes to play tag, but that's not one of my big interests. He's shared that last weekend his family went on a hike. I like to hike. I think I'll try that."

Sammy and I sit next to each other, pretending that we're in the lunchroom. "Sammy," I say, "what was that hike like that you were telling us about in Morning Meeting?"

"We went to Sleeping Giant State Park. I saw a hawk," Sammy responds.

"I love to hike at Sleeping Giant. I've seen hawks soaring over the peak, too," I say.

I turn to the class. "What did you notice about our play?"

Children have lots to say: "You and Sammy talked about the same thing." "When Sammy mentioned hawks, you did, too."

I turned to Sammy. "How did that feel?"

"It felt friendly," he answered.

"Who else would like to be in our play?" I ask. Lots of hands go up. I pick Manuel.

Now it's Sammy's turn to pick an idea from our chart. Sammy picks asking Manuel what he likes to do after school. "Manuel, what do you like to do after school?" Sammy asks.

"I like to shoot hoops," Manuel answers.

"I'm not so good at shooting hoops," Sammy answers. "Is there something we both like to do after school?"

"I like to bug my older brother while he tries to do his homework. You have an older brother, don't you?"

"Yup!" says Sammy. "I like to tease him, too."

"What did you notice?" I ask the class.

"Sammy and Manuel kept going until they found something that they both liked," says Michele.

"How did it feel?" I ask Sammy and Manuel.

"Friendly," they say in unison.

Later that day, Sammy actually asks Manuel to be his lunch partner. When I pick the students up in the lunchroom, I hear lots of friendly conversations going on.

Deepening our relationships through Morning Meetings

In September our Morning Meetings were full of activities designed to help us all get to know each other. Now, in November, it's time to learn more, to deepen our relationships.

Today as the children join the circle, I hand each child half of an addition flash card. The cards have been cut so that one half contains the two addends, the other half the sum. When the meeting begins, Frankie reads "6 | 7" from his card, and Zoe happily answers "13," the sum written on her card. Frankie and Zoe sit next to each other and greet each other with a friendly "Good morning." This process continues until everyone has a partner.

Now I give each partnership a piece of paper and a pencil. The paper is filled with two interlocking circles that create a Venn diagram. We've been studying Venn diagrams in math, so the children know that the center part is for things that the two circles have in common and the two outer parts are for things that are unique to each circle.

Each child labels his circle with his name. The pairs of children are to find out what they have in common and what's unique to each of them. But before they start, we brainstorm as a class the types of questions students might ask each other. Siblings, favorite foods, favorite TV shows, and what you like to do with your spare time all go on the list. The partners begin to talk. Glancing around, I see children deeply engaged in their conversations. I hear laughter and I see smiles.

Sammy and Jenny are partners. They probably wouldn't seek each other out, but with the magic of the random sort, they're happily getting to know each other. They discover that they both like to go on Penguin Club. I even hear them discussing "meeting" there.

We continue to enjoy this activity for the next two weeks, with students switching partners so they work with many classmates. Not surprisingly, they're becoming more and more adept at finding comfortable conversations for lunchtime.

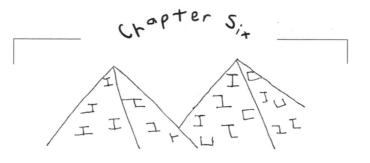

Chapter Six

The Passion Study

W e all have things that we're passionate about," I begin one November morning. "I'll bet you know some of the things I'm passionate about." By now the children know me well enough to know about my interests.

"You love mountains and mountain climbing," says Garret.

"You love nature and wild animals," adds Sophie.

"You love being a teacher," says Juan.

"You love us," chimes in Sammy.

"I'm going to choose one of my passions to study in depth," I say, "one that I'd like to learn more about. You're going to choose a passion to study, too, one that you'd like to learn more about. What are some of the things that you or your classmates are passionate about?"

"Mitsuke loves gymnastics," volunteers Michele.

"Garret loves grizzly bears," adds Paulina.

"Robert is interested in fishing," Frankie contributes.

The topic introduced, the children go back to their tables to brainstorm and discuss their passions with partners.

This passion study is something all the third grade classes are doing, and soon the building is abuzz with talk of passions. Our class interviews our principal about her passions: Italy and theater. Two of the third grade teachers create a bulletin board about the adult staff and their passions: Our paraprofessional, Mrs. Robinson, loves her grandchildren. Our PE teacher, Ms. Kamens, loves Jimmy Buffet. We're creating a context that says everyone has passions.

The children take their time choosing which passions they'll study. It's important that they choose something they'll be invested in for the duration of this research project.

In time, the students begin to make their choices. Lori is going to study horses. Robert will study submarines. Sammy knows right away that he wants to study history, but narrowing down that topic proves a challenge. He thinks about the Iroquois League of Nations, the U.S. Constitutional Convention, the life of Patrick Henry, ancient Egypt and the pyramids. The more topics he thinks of, the more frustrated he becomes.

At the end of the week, it's time to go to the library to begin our first research lesson with Ms. Lessler, our library media specialist. Each student needs a list of three potential topics for our lesson. Most children are so sure of one passion that it's hard for me to get them to list a second choice. Sammy, however, is still stuck on "I want to study everything about history. That's my passion."

I sit down with Sammy and list all the topics he's considering. I go down the list asking two questions about each item: "Are you interested in this topic?" and "Do you want to learn more about it?" We cross off the topics that he says he doesn't have a consuming interest in, such as the Constitutional Convention and the lives of Patrick Henry and Ben Franklin. The Iroquois League of Nations goes off the list because he already knows a lot about it and doesn't feel compelled to learn more. The topics that remain are World War II, the pyramids of ancient Egypt, and the destruction of Pompeii. A little one-on-one attention helped him pare his overwhelming list down to something manageable.

In the library lesson, Ms. Lessler teaches the children how to figure out whether there's sufficient information about a topic so they can choose a realistic topic from their lists of three. There isn't a lot of age-appropriate information about World War II, a little more about Pompeii, and lots about the pyramids of ancient Egypt. Sammy happily chooses that topic. Ms. Lessler has provided a structure that's helped him find his way out of his overwhelming maze of ideas. Again, Sammy is learning to be efficient.

Two weeks later, Sammy's fortress of books has turned into a gigantic inverted pyramid of resources about Egypt. The pyramid veers upward and outward, periodically tipping and scattering books onto Sammy's table and the surrounding floor. "Oh, no," I say, laughing. "This pyramid is definitely not a stairway to heaven." Sammy laughs, too. He knows I'm referring to his research finding that the pyramids may have been meant to be giant stairways taking the pharaoh into the afterlife above.

From my journal, December 14:

The passion project ought to be perfect for Sammy. It is, after all, a study of one of his passions, and who is more passionate about his passions than Sammy? Also, even more than most children, Sammy loves to have choices. For this study he had multiple choices of what to study. The powerful motivation of choice has impelled him forward in his research. He's read and learned voraciously. He now knows so much about the ancient Egyptians and their pyramids. He can discuss his knowledge with clarity and individual voice.

Organization: "I think I'll start a 'Do Not Lose' folder."

Sammy's gathered and absorbed lots of good information about his topic. Organizing it, however, is another story. Despite our step-by-step lessons on notetaking and keeping the notes in an easy-to-use system, Sammy's "organizer" is a combination of folded-over pages, crumpled papers, and sheets of his illegible scrawls. Some one-on-one attention would help him get his material in order, and consistent one-on-one attention would help him keep it that way.

But lots of students need my help on this project. More than half of the class is working pretty independently with the support of whole-class lessons, a graphic organizer I taught them to use, and brief check-ins with me. But as in any third grade class, several students are struggling. Garret needs help sorting the most important information about grizzlies (such as how many cubs they have over their lifetimes) from information that's interesting but less crucial to his research (such as "Once my mom saw a grizzly"). Sofia, stymied by words such as "marsupial" in her koala study, needs help with vocabulary. Patricia is thrown off by figurative language, thinking Leonardo da Vinci created a living, breathing monster when an author called one of the artist's creations a "monster."

With so many students needing my help, how can I give Sammy the help that he needs? All I can do right now is give him a sturdy nudge in the right direction.

I sit down with Sammy while the class is busily engaged with research. "Sammy," I say, "I can see that you've learned so much about the pyramids of ancient Egypt."

"Yup, I know a lot about Egypt now. Did you know that Hatshepsup was a woman who pretended to be a man pharaoh?"

I resist the temptation to pick up this fascinating conversational gambit, moving on instead to the topic I want to talk about. "I'm concerned that you're losing track of a lot of important information. How can you get your papers organized so that you know where they are?"

"I think I'll start a new folder," Sammy says in characteristic fashion. "I'll call it 'Do Not Lose,' and I won't lose it," he announces with a big smile. "Do you have any extra folders?"

I do, in fact, have some extra folders. I give him one with two pockets and metal fasteners to anchor hole-punched paper. He proudly writes "Do Not Lose" on it and starts to sort his mountain of papers, deciding what he needs and what he doesn't, what will go in the folder and what will go in the recycling.

I move on to work with other children. Sammy has a start at organization, but he'll clearly need more consistent follow-up than I can give him if he's to stay on track organizationally.

Ms. Lessler to the rescue

My dilemma about how to get more help for Sammy is solved when Ms. Lessler volunteers her services. Several coinciding events and scheduling conflicts have resulted in her library classes being canceled this week, so she announced that she was available to help any class with research. We in the third grade gratefully accepted.

Ms. Lessler and I share the job of teaching small-group lessons for children who need extra help with various research tasks. That clears some of my time to continue helping Sammy with organization. To his "Do Not Lose" folder system, I add assignments designed to help him sort and organize his thinking. I have him tell Mitsuke about the pyramids in a way that she can understand. For homework, he's to share his information with his mom. His research is gaining focus.

Partner troubles

The children are almost ready to present their learning from their passion studies. Just as they had a choice of research topic, they now have a choice of presentation format. They may write a report, give a dramatic presentation, build a model, make a poster, or create a fictional story. Today the children are rehearsing their final projects with table partners.

I hear loud complaints from Sammy's table.

"She's not listening to me! She's not listening to me!" Sammy screams.

"He's using words I don't understand," Jenny retorts.

"What did you say, Sammy?" I ask.

"I said 'The necropolis of Giza was full of pyramids, covered with gleaming limestone.'"

"I don't know what 'necropolis' means," protests Jenny.

"Even my baby cousin knows that 'necropolis' means 'city of the dead,'" Sammy complains. "He listened to me when I told him about my poster."

"Sammy, stop and look at our classroom rules," I say firmly and calmly.

Sammy looks at the rules and says to Jenny, "OK, I guess that wasn't a respectful thing to say, but you should have listened to me."

From my journal, December 18:

For many third graders, partner work is pure delight. After I introduce a lesson, hands fly up. "Do we get to work with partners today?" For Sammy, though, partner work is agony. He's so bright and eclectic that his vocabulary and his complex ideas are often above the heads of his classmates. When he works with a partner, his partner is often confused and thus inattentive. Sammy, in turn, is often inattentive and even downright rude. I can't give him the level of help in partner work that I can give him during whole-group lessons. There are eleven other pairs of students that I need to check in with while Sammy is ignoring or insulting his partner. Nonetheless, I need to figure out how to help him through this. I don't want to give up on helping him learn to work with a partner. I don't want to reinforce his difference from the rest of his classmates by having him work alone while they happily collaborate.

But which area of learning should Sammy work with a partner on? I need to prioritize here. He loves to read and has interesting things to say when he discusses books with me. He's had some recent breakthroughs in math problem-solving, but talking and writing about math is still a struggle for him. I don't want to layer that with the social demands of working with a partner. Writing fits into the same category. It's such a struggle for him to write alone that it's unrealistic to think he can collaborate here. I think I'll stick to teaching Sammy to work with a partner in his area of strength: reading.

Who would make a good reading partner for Sammy? Paul likes history and is, like Sammy, an extremely bright student. He won't be overwhelmed by Sammy's ideas or his vocabulary. Even though Paul and Sammy didn't do so well the first time I put them together, I believe there's something to build on there. I'll pair them up for a while, give them plenty of supervision, and as Sammy gains more partner skills, I'll try putting other classmates with him.

An efficient final project

For his final project, Sammy has decided to create a model of a pyramid with an accompanying poster. He's carefully labeling each part of the pyramid—the base, the steps, the apex, the reflective limestone facing. These simple labels represent a far greater output than he writes for his "letters home" journal. Apparently his deep interest in the topic is carrying him along, making writing less onerous. I wonder if I can use this high interest to encourage him to write some sentences.

I sit down next to him. "Sammy," I ask, "what are the most important things that you've learned about the pyramids?"

"They were tombs," he says, "for the pharaohs and their consorts. Some people think they were meant to take the pharaohs' souls to heaven."

"Sammy," I say, "that was an efficient statement!" referring back to our work in explaining his math problem-solving. "Would you like to try to write it on your poster?"

Sammy, confidence boosted through recalling his recent success with math work, quickly agrees and starts to record his thought. When I come back a few minutes later, he has written "The pyramids were tombs for the pharaohs. The pharaohs' souls were meant to climb up the steps to heaven."

Success! Sammy is pulling many of his newly gained skills together to create what promises to be a fascinating and easy-to-understand poster!

Presentations take three days, leading us right up to the December holiday break. Lori shares her giant labeled picture of a horse, full of rich information. Robert shows us his scale model of a submarine. Garret reads us the fictional story he wrote about grizzlies that includes all the information he gleaned through his research. Patricia dresses up as Leonardo da Vinci and tells the story of Leonardo's life using an "I" voice. Mitsuke shares her report about gymnastics. Last but not least, Sammy presents a detailed model of a pyramid, a model that opens up to show the sarcophagus of the pharaoh inside, surrounded by all of his material wealth. The accompanying poster includes rich information, delivered in efficient sentences and phrases. Sammy has truly mined his passions for this study, both in his choice of topic and in the way he's shown his learning.

> From my journal, December 22:
>
> I think Sammy and I are on to something with the concept of efficiency. I wonder if he's been feeling overwhelmed by the rush of complex ideas that fill his brain. When I elevated and honored the idea of efficiency, Sammy had permission to distill his complex information down to simple yet rich ideas that he could express in writing.

Which behaviors should I let go of?
Which behaviors should I firmly stop?

Sammy's behavior has come a long way. I'm using the RSC chair consistently for small misbehaviors (such as calling out in group lessons) before they become big problems. Sammy goes to the chair, takes a deep breath, sometimes squeezes the squeeze ball I gave him to keep his hands busy, and returns ready to listen. He's maintaining basic self-control in the group. What a change from the child who threw the Cuisenaire Rods at me the second day of school.

Other strategies for stopping misbehavior are helping, too. When Sammy starts to make pop-ups at inappropriate times, I take away those art materials for a brief but meaningful period of time.

Sammy longs for friends. He doesn't yet know how to connect with classmates. They're friendly to him, but he hasn't yet formed a close friendship with any of them. I'm holding firm to the expectation that he follow our classroom rule to respect and care for everyone. That will help him make friends. I'm using strategies such as whole-class role-plays to show everyone how to be friendly, respectful, and caring, and I'm using one-on-one coaching to teach Sammy social skills that the other children already have.

I let some of Sammy's behaviors slide. I don't expect him to sit perfectly still during group lessons or during Morning Meeting. That's just not realistic. I do expect him to keep his hands and feet off other children, to stay out of the middle of the circle, and to avoid other behaviors that distract his classmates.

Since his table's conflict resolution meeting about his pop-ups, Sammy's been keeping his overflow on a shelf near his seat. We change seats every two weeks using a random card sort, yet Sammy keeps ending up in the same place with an ever-changing cast of tablemates. Is he switching cards with classmates so he can keep ending up at the "three" table? I can't go on pretending that I don't notice this irregularity.

When I ask Sammy about this—in a curious rather than accusing voice, as tone is everything—Sammy says, "I need that table. There's room for my books on the shelf. That way the kids at my table won't get mad because I'm taking up too much space. Can I have a three card every time we change tables, pleeeeease?"

I agree to his request because it's reasonable. He's thinking about what he needs for success in school. Since I've decided to let him continue to bring his big red duffle bagfuls of books, he needs the space.

And I see no need to delve into how he has managed to stay at the three table so consistently. My guess is that other kids are giving him their three cards because they know how helpful the extra space is to him. They understand that we all need different things. Fair isn't always the same as equal.

Academically, Sammy's participating fully in math, reading, science, social studies, and handwriting. Composing his ideas in writing continues to be an issue, although he made small gains in the passion project. I know that Sammy, like all children, wants to succeed in school. I know children do the best they can. It's up to me to find the key that will unlock Sammy's ability to compose his creative thoughts in writing. Perhaps the idea of efficiency will continue to help. Above all, I need to keep being his ally and keep my strategies positive so that writing doesn't turn into a power struggle.

Sammy marches to his own drummer. I don't want to make him just like everyone else; I want him to be the unique and wonderful person that he is. My goal for him is that he'll learn to contain some of his less socially acceptable behaviors so he can make friends. My goal for myself is that I'll respect his needs while I respect the entire group's right to learn.

PART 3

GROWTH IN THE NEW YEAR

January through March

Chapter Seven

Easing Back into the Rhythms of School

Slush is heavy in the school driveway and snow is falling as the school busses pull up in front of the school. Children chatter animatedly on this first day back from December break, bumping and giggling their way down the hall. Robert snatches Max's hat away; Max grabs it back. Their rough-and-tumble play, like puppies, reminds me that many of them have spent the past week playing outside in the snow.

As they enter our classroom, the children are full of stories about their holiday break. "Ms. Crowe, Ms. Crowe, look at my new book!" exclaims Sammy. It's a thick volume about Native Americans, full of maps, illustrations, and text. "That's going to come in handy," I reply. "Pretty soon we'll start our study of the Native Americans of the Eastern Woodlands. I'll bet that book will help you."

The students still have one foot in December vacation and, to tell the truth, so do I. My goal for our first Morning Meeting after the holiday is to reconnect in a low-stress way. We greet each other using the "one-minute mix and mingle." *How many classmates can you greet in one minute?* It's perfect for reconnecting briefly with many classmates after some time away.

For Morning Meeting sharing, we form two concentric circles, the inner circle facing out and the outer circle facing in so pairs of children face each other. We tell our partners something we enjoyed about our vacations, and then everyone takes a step to the right and talks to a new partner. For Morning Meeting activity, we play a couple of quick rounds of Coseeki, a familiar clapping and gesturing game. We bond through the power of lighthearted fun.

How we want school to be in the new year

Later on, at social studies time, we sit together in a circle. "Close your eyes," I say to the class, "and think about how you want school to be in the new year. What are you hoping to learn? What might make school safe and fun for you and for your classmates? Make a picture in your mind. Put yourself there. What do you see? What do you hear? What are you doing? What are you saying?" I ask each question slowly, giving the students plenty of time to reflect and imagine.

"Now open your eyes. If you'd like, tell the person sitting next to you what you pictured in your mind."

We've been together long enough that I'm relatively certain the children will feel safe with this possibly intimate sharing. I do, however, give them the option to be a listener, just in case it doesn't feel safe to some. Few, if any, take this option. The circle is full of children talking, telling each other about playing with friends and learning their multiplication tables.

"Now let's take a look at our rules," I say. "Remember how hard we worked on them in September? How might our rules help our class to be the way we all want school to be in the coming year? Take some time to think privately." After a few minutes, I ask, "Would someone like to share?"

Jenny tells us that she wants to learn her multiplication tables really, really well and that our rule "Listen and do your best work" will help her. Robert wants to learn how to play chess so that he can play that game with Max on indoor recess days. He thinks that both "Listen and do your best work" and "Respect and care for everyone" will help him achieve his goal.

Next I bring out a chart with our rules listed and spaces under each rule. Children tell me which of our rules will help them particularly, and I write their names under those rules. I then organize the children into groups of four according to which rules their names are under. Each group's job is to plan a short play about how their rule will help students.

Sammy longs for a friend

As the children get into their groups, Sammy whispers to me, "I want a friend."

I feel simultaneously sad and hopeful hearing this. "Which rule will help?" I whisper back to Sammy. "Respect and care for everyone," he replies, and then goes off to work with his group.

I'm sad because he wants a friend so badly, yet it's so hard for him to make friends. At the same time, I'm hopeful because we have structures in this classroom to help him behave in ways that encourage classmates to warm to him. And he's starting to change: With coaching, he is now more able to do some friendly give-and-take with peers.

Today I've purposely put him in a slightly smaller group, with just Marie and Paul. That way Marie's special education paraprofessional, Ms. Jones, can help Sammy focus on the task at hand.

After the class has been working for a while, I glance over at Sammy's group. Sammy is starting to dig in his heels about a decision the group is trying to make. "But I want our play to take place in the lunchroom." Ms. Jones, a graduate student studying special education, gently urges him to think about how his ideas would look and sound if they took place on the playground, since that is Paul and Marie's setting of choice. Sammy actually does think about it and accedes to Marie and Paul's wishes.

There has been progress since those early days of school in September.

Reinforce, remind, redirect

I continue to use the three Rs of teacher language—reinforcing, reminding, and redirecting language—to work with Sammy, just as I use it with all the students. Sammy responds well when I use these three Rs well.

Reinforcing language

With lots of coaching and practice, Sammy has learned to sit in the circle successfully for more or less the entire twenty minutes of our Morning Meetings. Today was an example of this attentive participation. Sitting next to me, he paid attention for most of the meeting. "Sammy, you did it again," I whisper privately afterward to reinforce his behavior. "You listened to Lori share about her visit to her grandma and you asked her a question about her news." I name exactly and explicitly what he's doing well. That way he knows and can repeat his successes.

It helps that these meetings aren't longer than twenty minutes. I keep whole-group lessons short, too—no more than fifteen minutes. That way everyone listens. Even adults have difficulty attending at peak alertness for more than twenty minutes.

I reinforce appropriate social behaviors throughout the rest of the day as well. "I noticed you asking Paul to play at recess today," I say to Sammy in a private moment. "Paul wants a friend. You were following our rule to care for everyone." Sammy beams. We all enjoy recognition when we do something well, especially when the recognition is specific and targeted at behaviors related to our personal goals.

Reminding language

Like most teachers, I'm in the habit of giving students reminders. Before we step out into the corridor, I say, "Quiet in the hall. Remember, Ms. Pierce's class is working." Before recess, I say, "Remember, safe and kind playing at recess."

Sammy needs these whole-class reminders and reminders individualized just for him before he starts on a task. "You're going to be working with partners this morning at writing time," I tell him quietly. "Remember how we practiced listening to your partner and responding to what she says?" "Yup," he replies. "I will listen to her so I know what to say back."

He also needs reminders as he begins to get off track. I check in on Sammy and Mitsuke as she shares her writing with him. "Did I describe my setting clearly?" she asks him.

"I like stories about history," he replies.

"Remember what we talked about," I whisper to Sammy. "What did Mitsuke ask for feedback on?"

"Could you read the part that describes your setting again?" he asks Mitsuke politely.

Sometimes, using the RSC chair to stop misbehavior early on is more appropriate than issuing a reminder. Robert shares in Morning Meeting about sledding on the hill in back of our school with his dad. This makes Sammy think of the time he went sledding with his dad, and he loudly interrupts, "I sled with my dad, too. My dad gave me a big push and …"

"RSC, Sammy," I say quietly and calmly. The class has been taught and has practiced listening without interrupting. They've even practiced keeping the focus on the sharer when giving comments rather than injecting their own story. Sammy forgot these rules in a moment of excitement, and the RSC helps children remember in such instances. Sammy heads off to the RSC chair, and Robert continues with his sharing. Sammy sits in the chair for a minute, collects himself, then rejoins the group and listens respectfully to the questions his classmates are asking Robert.

Redirecting language

These days, when Sammy starts on some activity or project that's out of sync with the class or otherwise inappropriate, my redirection, delivered calmly, firmly, and promptly before he's too far gone, can usually get him back on track.

It's a snowy January day and we're well into the rather lengthy preparation needed for recess. Most students have their snow pants and boots on. I look around the room and notice Sammy still curled up in a corner, reading a book about the Constitutional Convention. "Sammy, snow pants and boots on now," I say firmly and calmly. He scrambles for his gear and is soon straggling down the hall at the end of the line. Sammy and I have certainly made progress since his field trip meltdown in the fall.

From my journal, January 12:

Complacency can become my nemesis if I'm not careful. Now, in January, it seems that Sammy has made so much progress since September. It would be easy to take this improvement for granted, yet I know I need to push myself to remember to congratulate him on his frequent successes. His self-control is still tenuous. It would be all too easy for him to fall back into old behaviors and patterns. My reinforcements are helping the new behaviors stick. No matter how tempted I am to breathe a sigh of relief and say, "Whew, that's done!" and focus on other things, I know if I start to do that, his efforts will begin to unravel.

And then there's the matter of redirection. When Sammy chooses his direction, he can become like a giant ocean liner, committed to his course, unable to turn. That's why it's so important to redirect him early, before he's so committed that it's too late.

Remembering to step back and observe

Observing students every day, all year long, is so important. Midyear, especially, is a time to step back and take stock of progress so far. How have the students grown? Where are they stuck? What can I do to help each of them?

Paul is progressing in math. He knows his multiplication facts through the five tables. I see a smile of self-confidence on his face as he plays "Race to 100" and places the base ten block correctly. Jenny's more accepting that she needs to read books of a level she can handle, and thus her reading has improved. Halima's homework is sliding seriously. I think my first step will be to speak to one of her family members about it.

Sammy, I observe, is making progress in writing, which has been an area of such struggle for him. I see an example of this in our preparations for standardized testing.

On the day of the test, the children will be writing a story on an assigned topic. To help them feel relaxed about this type of assignment, so different from anything they've done before in school, we have a few low-stress practice experiences, using prompts from past years' tests. I tell the children that they're each going to write a story about taking care of a neighbor's pet. I give them some time to think. Then I assign them partners with whom to share their ideas and talk through their story.

I walk by Sammy and Paul just in time to hear Sammy tell a humorous fictional story about his mother agreeing to adopt an additional dog into the family because she was in the shower and couldn't hear his question accurately. He accepts this pre-writing stage of talking about his ideas to get them flowing, and his sense of humor serves him well as he talks. When it's time to write, Sammy gets a few sentences down on the paper. He smiles as he grips the pencil tightly. He's slowly becoming more comfortable with writing. It helps that he actually likes the test prep practice, which is so much more structured than some of our other writing experiences.

When it comes to reading, Sammy, though an avid reader, can be stretched to expand into new territory. I often see Sammy absorbed in a nonfiction book. He's tried a fiction book or two at my urging, though they haven't been his favorites. I thought he'd love the outdoor adventure *Hatchet*, by Gary Paulsen, a survival tale of a boy alone in the wilderness. He read dutifully when I was close by, but as soon as I turned to work with another student, he picked up one of his history books, far more alluring to him than fiction. I think I'll try to interest him next in *Sign of the Beaver* by Elizabeth George Speare, a historical fiction survival story about a boy in colonial times. The colonial setting and the excitement of a boy alone in a cabin all winter, his life saved by a Native American boy who helps him, should capture Sammy's interest.

In math, Sammy not only solves problems successfully but eagerly shares his ideas in group discussions. "I'm noticing the way the angles of the polygons relate," he says. "When one angle gets larger (more obtuse) another gets smaller (more acute)." He's trying out new vocabulary. When asked, he'll happily say, "I like math." Learning his multiplication facts is another matter. When I tell him that I'm ready to hear his multiplication facts, his responses range from, "Hunh?" to "Well … , maybe tomorrow." Other children are invested in this rite of passage but Sammy appears to be unconcerned.

Report cards are due at the end of January. They're a great opportunity to use my observations and also to reflect about each child. "Sammy loves to learn," I write on his report card. "He enjoys sharing his creative ideas with the class during whole-class lessons." What growth, I think to myself. It wasn't long ago that Sammy struggled to sit with the group and, back then, when he attempted to share his ideas with the class, the kids often didn't understand him as he wandered around the idea.

Working with peers: Arguing and scaring other children

One area in which Sammy has improved less is working with peers. As I wrote on his report card, "Small group work is harder for Sammy. He becomes frustrated when other children don't understand his ideas and has yet to learn the skill of listening to his peers' ideas. I often find myself intervening to help resolve explosive conflicts as Sammy and his group try to solve an academic problem."

That's the challenge: to help Sammy work more successfully with peers during those times when I'm not close at hand coaching and supporting.

The children are working in small groups on a geometry challenge. They're creating polygons out of triangles. *How many different ways can you arrange four congruent triangles so that each triangle has at least one edge that meets with another triangle edge, corners touching?*

Max, John, and Sammy are working together. Sammy has an idea for a new arrangement. Max and John are quite sure that it's a repeat of one that the group has already found. While working with Jenny and Paulina, I look across the room in time to see Sammy, red faced, start arguing with his group mates. "No! No! No!" he shouts at John and Max. By the time I get to their group, Sammy is beyond the point where he can discuss the math issue calmly. "Sammy, RSC," I say and he goes off to regain self-control. After a while, he gets up, gets a drink of water, and resumes work on the math problem, this time independently.

The next day we're sitting in the circle, sharing solutions to the four-triangle problem. Sammy, still absorbed in the unique solution that caused his explosion with Max and John yesterday, waves his paper with animation and determination. He rushes across the circle to show me his paper, stepping hard on Paulina's leg and then bowling her over. Paulina's face shows more than a little fear. I send Sammy to RSC while comforting Paulina.

A problem-solving conference: How to behave so kids will want to be friends

Sammy's behavior has improved in so many areas, and I can see that he can change. Some of his actions, however, are still getting in the way of achieving his heart's desire: friends who want to work and play with him. This is a topic that we need to address privately—he would be mortified if anyone overheard such a conference. So I ask Sammy to join me for lunch.

We sit at the reading table, each with our sandwich. "Sammy," I say, "you've learned to be respectful of other kids in so many ways. Remember last week when you listened respectfully to Lori when she shared in Morning Meeting about her grandma?"

"Yup," Sammy replies. "In second grade I didn't listen to other kids, and now I do."

"I think your classmates appreciate that," I say, "but I have noticed some behaviors that make it hard for them to enjoy working with you. Remember your argument with Max and John yesterday?"

"But I was right and they were wrong," Sammy remonstrates. "There was another solution to the problem."

"Sammy, we can look later and figure out if your polygon and another polygon from your group were congruent. For now, we need to talk about the way you responded when you disagreed. Remember the way you shouted 'No, no, no'?"

Sammy looks puzzled. "I don't really remember," he says.

I have noticed that when Sammy reaches the point where he's totally out of control, he often doesn't remember it later. This fact is such a window into the way his nonrational brain takes over in his most highly charged states.

Taking another tack, I say, "Remember yesterday when you stepped on Paulina in the circle?" Stepping on Paulina was a less emotional moment.

"Yup, I remember that. I didn't see her."

"But you scared her," I say. Then, to move the conversation away from what I've noticed, I ask, "What have you noticed, Sammy, about how things are going when you work with your classmates?" I'm attempting a dialogue about how things are going, not a monologue by me about what's wrong with Sammy's behavior.

"You know it's hard for me," he says. "But yesterday I listened to Mitsuke when she was my writing partner. I helped her with the setting in her writing. And when Robert shared at Morning Meeting about sledding with his dad, I listened to him." Even though my goal is to help Sammy get along better with peers when I'm not around, I don't see any point in mentioning that each of these successes had been, in part, the result of my reminders. I'm happy to hear him name partial successes—they're great starts for us to build on.

Sammy continues, "When we made our wishes about the new year, you know I wished for friends."

So, there it is. Sammy raised the issue himself. He sees that his behaviors are getting in the way of making true friends.

"How can I help you with these behaviors so that kids will want to work with you?" I ask. I want to be his ally. I know it's hard for him, in the heat of the moment, to be aware of and control his behaviors that might affect other students' attitudes toward him. He reacts and then he's in over his head.

"You know the sign language sign for 'R'?" he responds. "You could use it when you see me doing something that might scare other kids or make them mad. You know, 'R' for 'reminder'."

"OK," I reply. "Let's try that." I'm not wildly optimistic that giving him a reminder like this will turn around his alienating behavior with classmates. After all, the biggest problem is his inability to control his impulsiveness when I'm not available to give him reminders. But I sense this new reminder system is as far as Sammy's able to go for now. I want to build our mutual sense of collaboration by going with Sammy's idea. That way he'll be invested in making it work.

Sammy and I walk downstairs to pick up the other students from lunch. As we enter the cafeteria, Sammy makes a beeline for our class's tables and loudly announces, "Don't anyone ask me why I had a special meeting with Ms. Crowe. It's private."

Later in the week I start off writers' workshop with a mini-lesson reviewing how to give a partner feedback about the area that she asks for help in. The children write for twenty minutes and then get together in pairs.

As they head off to meet with their partners, I say, "Remember, feedback that your partner asks for." As Sammy walks across the room to meet with Marie, I give him a sign language R-for-reminder. Sammy nods at me. Later on I hear Sammy politely asking Marie, "What would you like help with?" The R-for-reminder seems to have helped him remember his goal in working with Marie. We'll see how well it works for pulling his behavior back on track when he's already in the middle of some emotionally charged situation.

Chapter Eight

Progress in "the Friends Department"

It's February and still snowing. At recess, groups of children build snow forts, make impromptu sleds with cardboard from home, and try surreptitiously to pack snow balls. They are absorbed.

Today I notice Sammy standing by himself. "What's up?" I ask him.

"The other kids won't play with me," he says.

"Have you tried to join them?"

"Well, no. They only do dumb things like making snow forts."

"Sammy, it sounds to me like you're the one who won't play with them," I say as gently as I can. "If you want to play with other kids, I think you need to pick something that they're doing and join them. You could say, 'May I play?' or, even better, you could just start playing, joining in with what they're already doing."

A few minutes later, I notice Sammy in the midst of a group of about twenty children, creating a giant snow fort.

As the third graders line up to walk inside, I say to Sammy, "I noticed you joining the group at the snow fort. Which strategy did you try?"

"I just started making a wall," he told me with a smile.

"Jenny's mean to me"

Despite successes like joining in to make the snow fort, getting along with peers continues to be a challenge for Sammy. In any class of third graders, there're bound to be small misunderstandings among the students. But for Sammy, given his difficulty with social skills, these misunderstandings build up in his imagination until they're out-of-control crises.

As I pick up the class from PE, the PE teacher pulls me aside. "What's going on with Sammy?" she asks. "I partnered him up with Jenny, and he flatly refused to work with her. He tantrumed, kicked and screamed, shouted 'I can't work with her!'" I thank her for telling me and say that I'll talk with Sammy.

Later in the morning, while the other students are silent reading, I have a moment to meet privately with Sammy at the reading table.

"What happened at PE?" I ask in a neutral tone.

"She tried to make me work with Jenny. Jenny's mean to me."

"Oh? What did Jenny do?" I ask, exploring.

"Kids tell me she takes my stuff."

"Have you ever seen her take your stuff?" I probe.

"Well … , no."

"So why do you believe it?" Investigating further, I continue, "Which kids told you?"

"I don't remember," Sammy replies, looking genuinely confused.

"I think it's time for a Peace Talk with Jenny," I say. "That way you two can talk about this together."

The class has been practicing "Peace Talks," our name for conflict resolution meetings, informally all year under my supervision. Since returning from holiday break, I've been teaching specific lessons on how to have a formal Peace Talk with a classmate without my supervision. Lots of children are having such meetings independently now. But I think Sammy, with his limited social skills, would do better talking with Jenny while I watch, ready to coach him if needed.

The Peace Talk: "I don't like it when you take my stuff."

"First you need to invite Jenny to the Peace Talk," I say to Sammy. "What are you going to say to her?"

Sammy looks up at our Peace Talk chart on the wall. The chart lists the steps in a Peace Talk.

"Jenny, I have an I-statement for you," he says.

"And what will you then say for your I-statement?"

Looking at the chart again, he says, "I don't like it when you take my stuff."

Sammy walks over to Jenny, who's sprawled out on the floor reading a Judy Moody book. "Jenny, I have an I-statement for you," Sammy announces.

"OK," she says, looking surprised. After the tantrum in PE today, she may very well be thinking that she ought to be the one with the I-statement for him.

Together they walk to the spot behind the chart stand, our official Peace Talk spot. I sit nearby, ready to step in if needed. From a basket, they each take out a card that lists our Peace Talk ground rules. The children know that every Peace Talk begins with the partners taking turns reading the rules aloud. "Listen to your partner," reads Sammy. "Work to solve the problem," reads Jenny.

Glancing up at the chart to stay on track with the steps, Sammy delivers his I-statement: "Jenny, I don't like it when you take my stuff."

Jenny looks even more surprised than before and starts to blurt out a remonstrance. She stops herself, though, and, quickly glancing at the chart of steps, remembers that her job is first to paraphrase what Sammy said. "I hear you say that you don't like it when I take your stuff." Sammy nods to show that she's restated his words correctly. Jenny then states, "I don't take your stuff."

"OK, so you don't take my stuff," Sammy repeats. He, too, remembers that his job is also to paraphrase before asserting his own point. Sammy actually accepts Jenny's statement, but then he goes down another line of thinking. "But you're friends with Lexi, and Lexi takes my stuff."

"Sammy, I feel hurt and angry when you blame me for something that you think Lexi did," replies Jenny.

"I hear you say you don't like it when I blame you for taking my stuff when Lexi is the one who takes my things," says Sammy.

This is getting complicated. I send Sammy off to get Lexi.

When Lexi joins the talk, Sammy says, "Lexi, I don't like it when you take my stuff."

Lexi gets a look of surprise on her face similar to Jenny's. "I hear you say that you don't like it when I take your stuff. But I don't take your stuff," she says.

"You're saying that you don't take my stuff. Remember last week when you were my writing partner? After you sat at my table, some of my special pop-ups were missing and someone told me that you took them," Sammy says.

"So, you think I took your pop-ups. Sometimes Ms. Crowe says to clean up and your stuff is all over the table. You don't clean up and so I have to. Maybe I moved your pop-up, but I don't like it when I have to do your cleanup."

"Alright," says Sammy. "I'll try to be part of cleanup."

"Maybe that missing pop-up is over on your special shelf," suggests Lexi.

Sure enough, the pop-up is on the shelf. Some measure of peace is restored.

From my journal, February 3:

The Peace Talk has provided me with new insights into Sammy's world view. Does he see the world as divided into two groups? I've been seeing things that point toward that way of thinking ever since September when he wrote THE KDS BOTHRD ME about second grade. There are intimate, loyal friends (or hoped-for friends) like Max and untrustworthy classmates such as Jenny and Lexi. In this way of thinking, Jenny and Lexi are almost one unit, the type of unit that he would like to be with Max. If Lexi takes my stuff, and Jenny is Lexi's friend, then Jenny must take my stuff, too. That was his logic. I hope today's Peace Talk helped him see the error in this line of reasoning.

Passing during the compliment circle

Every Friday afternoon, a half hour before dismissal, our class gathers on the rug for a compliment circle in which the children name helpful things they've seen classmates doing the past week. This is a practice I learned from a colleague early in my career. When carefully taught, compliment circles, even occasional ones, can dramatically alter the whole atmosphere of the group, bringing a sense of warmth and caring to our classroom community. As a student of mine once wrote, "Compliment circles make everyone feel good."

Of course, to build community, it's important that everyone is complimented and that individuals compliment a variety of classmates, not just one special friend. I've carefully taught the class that this is our goal. I've also taught the specifics of how to give and receive compliments, and we've been practicing since the fall.

Today, Paul starts us off by saying, "Patricia, I'd like to thank you for helping me with my writing this week." "You're welcome," Patricia replies. Then it's her turn to deliver a compliment. "Juan, thank you for remembering to greet people who got to school late," she say. Next it's Juan's turn.

The expectation is that everyone will receive a compliment. Early in the year, I keep a list and make sure that I compliment the children who didn't get recognized by their peers. As the year progresses, I begin to ask the class, "Who hasn't been complimented yet today?" As children raise their hands, classmates look around and eagerly volunteer to help out with a friendly compliment.

"Sammy, thank you for agreeing to help more at cleanup," says Lexi. "You pitched right in today." Sammy is often the recipient of these slightly backhanded but ultimately sincere compliments. Inevitably, some children are easy to compliment, and others are more of a challenge. Sammy is hard to compliment. And he has an even harder time complimenting someone else. Once Lexi thanks Sammy, it's Sammy's turn to compliment someone, but instead he says "Pass." Passers get to select another student who will give a compliment, and Sammy picks Pua.

I suspect Sammy is so central to his own universe, as a younger student might be, that he's not yet able to be observant of other students' behaviors.

Meeting the Valentine compliments challenge, eventually

Valentine's Day will be here in less than two weeks. Rather than marking the day with candy and packs of commercial Valentine cards, I prefer to use the day to celebrate our community. I give each child a class list. The children's job, their homework for the week, is to write a brief compliment about each classmate. The children have had six months of practice in giving compliments, but now the standard is raised: They need to come up with an individual compliment for everyone.

We discuss how to notice classmates, even how to jot down thoughts when they see someone doing something helpful for a student or the group. We discuss how to be aware of behaviors that classmates might miss. For example, we all know that Michele is good at math, and it would be easy to compliment her for her math skill. But I encourage students to stretch themselves and observe another positive thing in Michele, a way that she helps others.

On the morning of February 10, I open my email to find a message from Sammy's mother. "Sammy couldn't do his homework," she writes. "He had a really hard time coming up with anything positive to say about any classmates. Some of the statements that he did write were kind of sad, like 'You sit with me even if no one else will.'" As I read her email I hear her concern that Sammy may feel alone and rejected.

I call Mrs. Smith. First off, I reassure her. "Sammy's classmates work with him," I say. "Yesterday he and Manuel were reading partners. He sat with Garret at lunch, and at recess he played with a big group making a snow fort on the playground." I try to be as specific as possible.

Next I describe Sammy's social issue in school simply, positively, and honestly. "I've been working with Sammy to help him join in with other children at recess. For a while he was reluctant and told me that the other kids only do 'dumb things,' but for the past week he's been joining the big group of children who play in the snow. He still needs a lot of support from me in order to work successfully with a partner or a small group. I've been coaching him on how to listen to classmates." It's important that I tell her what I'm doing to improve the situation—it reassures her that Sammy is getting the help he needs.

"I'll meet with Sammy today," I add. "I'll see if I can help him get started on his Valentine compliments."

Later, Marie's paraprofessional, Ms. Jones, and I sit down with Sammy while the other children are at music class. I asked Ms. Jones to help us because she's at recess and lunch every day and thus has had lots of opportunities to see Sammy interact socially in informal, less structured parts of the day than classroom times.

As soon as Sammy sees the compliment sheet, he announces, "I can't do this. I've already tried."

I push on because it's important that Sammy complete this assignment. Children will mark him socially if they receive compliments from everyone except him, and that would be a major step backward in his quest to gain friends. "Sammy," I say calmly and matter-of-factly, "how are kids going to feel about you if they see that they have a compliment from everyone except you?" Sammy puts his head down on the table.

It's that black-and-white vision again. Sammy's so busy seeing social relationships as love and hate, friends and enemies, that he isolates himself. Having labeled nearly everyone in the class an enemy (even as he wants desperately to convert them to friends), he's unable to see any positives in them.

"Sammy, Ms. Jones and I will help you, but this assignment needs to get done," I tell him.

Ms. Jones picks up the thread. "Sammy, remember how Paul was your partner in PE yesterday? Remember how he asked you if you wanted the first turn with the ball?" I type while Ms. Jones prods, and soon the compliments flow. Sammy manages to thank Max and John for listening to his ideas in their math group, despite some grumbling because they hadn't agreed with his idea. Even Lexi and Jenny, beside whose names Sammy had written a big "I" for "impossible," receive compliments for their work in the Peace Talk last week.

With gentle coaxing, Sammy is actually able to see positive things that classmates did for him in the past few weeks, and he seems to feel genuine appreciation once he's able to realign his perspective.

On Valentine's Day Sammy proudly passes out his compliments. He receives compliments from his classmates and pastes them each on a big red heart labeled "Sammy."

From my journal, February 14:

Early in my career, a colleague told me that if we can get kids to act in certain ways, their attitudes can follow along and actually be shaped by their actions. It seemed preposterous at the time, and yet over the years I've seen that to be true. When Sammy found himself noticing helpful things that classmates had done, it actually helped him feel friendly toward them.

I'm grateful that I was able to call on Ms. Jones here. As carefully as I try to notice students, I see them most fully in academic and structured social settings. Our colleagues who supervise lunch, recess, and boarding the school busses have a unique and valuable perspective.

The eraser Leonardos

A couple of weeks after Valentine's Day, I notice Sammy in animated conversation at his table, bobbing an eraser up and down. I walk over to see him performing a puppet show for his table, using small objects as puppets. As I get closer I realize that the small objects are four of the brand new erasers that I'd put aside for upcoming standardized testing. Each eraser now has a little face drawn on it. "Meet Leonardo," says Sammy proudly, a big grin on his face.

Fresh supplies are a valuable commodity in our school. I'd carefully ordered the exact amount that we'd need for testing out of my limited supply budget and was counting on being able to give each student a beautiful clean eraser to use during testing. My heart sinks when I see what Sammy's done. Struggling to preserve my own self-control, I say, "Sammy, where did you get the erasers?"

"I found them!" he exclaims happily.

"Those are the erasers that we'll need next week. You need to figure out how you can get them cleaned up so that we can use them."

"Can I keep one Leonardo?" asks Sammy. "That one can be my eraser."

"OK," I reply, "as long as you clean the other erasers so your tablemates will be able to use them."

During math I suddenly realize that Sammy has acquired another four "Leonardos," a friendship gift from Paul, who created them from his table's testing erasers. The floodgates are opening, and I suddenly foresee all of the erasers disappearing in a torrent of Leonardos. I ask Sammy and Paul to join me at the reading table.

"Sammy and Paul," I say, "which rule might help us take care of the erasers so that we have them for testing?"

"Take care of our environment," Sammy says.

"We need to use them for erasing, not Leonardos," says Paul.

"You two will spend some time during 'choice' cleaning the erasers," I say. "And no more puppets out of our class's erasers.

From my journal, February 28:

The eraser event was frustrating for me. I guess it's an indication that my level of tension is rising as testing approaches. I want to keep the testing experience as positive as it can be. Yet I have so little control over those two weeks. I'm focused on some details that I hope I can control, some of the material aspects of how to keep things pleasant, like shiny new erasers, clean and sharpened number-two pencils, and special snacks each day when the testing period is over. I need to take a deep breath here and think about what is most important (the children, not the erasers) and what is going well.

I'm using so many strategies with Sammy. They've become second nature for me. A look, a word, a quick direction to go to RSC—Sammy more and more often responds to these continual supports without objection. His behavior is falling more into line with classroom expectations. Even his misbehaviors with the erasers indicate positive change. Rather than making creations for himself alone, he was entertaining his tablemates. Paul was eager to be part of the entertainment, and Sammy drew Paul in. Such behaviors signal improved social skills and increased inclusion in our classroom community.

A friend he's not even aware of

Test prep is intensifying. We practice doing some test-like worksheets with everyone sitting in rows, quiet, just the way it will be during the real tests. Our assistant principal offers to take the children who, because of various special needs, will be taking their tests separately from the other students. Sammy and Michele are among this group. Ironically, these are students identified as "needing more time" to complete their tests although they're the ones who announce "I'm done" very shortly into the test. Separating them from the class mostly serves the purpose of keeping the classroom silent so that their classmates can concentrate more fully.

After the test practice I chat briefly with our assistant principal. "After about a half hour, Sammy and Michele were busy standing on their heads, rolling on the floor of my office, and passing each other silly notes," she tells me. "You know, those two have a lot in common. They really are friends," she says.

From my journal, March 2:

Sammy wishes for friends, talks about his lack of friends, yet he does have friends that he's not entirely aware of. He likes to work with Michele. He likes to play with her too, sending her silly notes and acting goofy together. I find it reassuring that he's making social connections with Michele, but he's still longing for something more. Michele just doesn't fit into his ideal of a friend. For one thing, she's a girl and he wants a boy to be his friend. For another, Michele has lots of friends and Sammy wants an exclusive friend. What's it going to take for him to recognize relationships with classmates like Michele as friendships?

Relationships with Other Adults

Our days go much more smoothly now, in the second half of the year. Sammy and I have a strong connection, which I maintain with a steady stream of reinforcements, reminders, redirections, and use of the RSC chair. These strategies require a constant but comfortably manageable flow of energy on my part, leaving me with time and space to work with all of the students. I'm able to help Paul with his math and Jenny with her reading. I've talked with Halima's mom about Halima's homework, and as a result her homework has become more consistent.

So, my relationship with Sammy is helping him steadily improve his self-control. That just goes to show what educators have long known: that a strong teacher–student relationship is key to children's success in school. But for Sammy, this currently means that he tends to fall apart when another adult is teaching the class.

Meltdown with the guest teacher

I'm out of the classroom for a few hours at a team meeting. The children are with a substitute teacher, a "guest teacher," as they're known in our school. There's a knock on the conference room door. It's the school psychologist, asking if I'd join her in her office for a few minutes. I walk into her office to see Sammy, sobbing and out of control, kicking the wall, screaming, "No! No! No!"

Apparently the children had lined up in the hall to walk to PE. Ms. Jones, Marie's paraprofessional, noticed that Sammy wasn't in line and checked the classroom. She found him in the art area, creating a puppet of Thomas Jefferson out of paper and a Popsicle stick. As Ms. Jones herded Sammy into line, she said, "Give me the puppet. You may have it back after PE."

Sammy responded by pleading, "No, please no, just let me have it for PE."

"You need your whole body for PE. Puppets are for later," Ms. Jones responded, using the type of consistent firm language that she'd heard me use.

Sammy was forging ahead by then, as unlikely to turn as the Titanic steaming toward its fateful iceberg. "No! No! No! No!" he screamed.

Ms. Jones gently guided him to the psychologist's office. Luckily Dr. Fischer was in her office and available. As I entered the psychologist's office I could see that Sammy was still deeply out of control as he continued to scream "No! No! No! No!" at Dr. Fischer.

"Sammy," I say, "let's take a walk." As we head down the hall to the water fountain, his sobs subside.

"The puppet is my friend," he tells me.

"Puppet friends are for the classroom. You can keep Thomas Jefferson on your table if he doesn't distract you or your tablemates from school work," I state as we walk together to pick up the class at PE.

This is not the only instance of Sammy's troubles with other adults. Early March is flu season, and despite my flu shot, I'm unexpectedly out sick for a day. I return the next day to find a long letter from Ms. Greene, the guest teacher, about Sammy's behavior. He hid behind the bookshelves, crawled under the tables, and screamed "No!" at her whenever she tried to intervene. It's been a long time since he's acted this way. My hypothesis, that he needs my consistent support to maintain self-control, is reinforced.

From my journal, March 7:

Sammy's increased self-control, sense of safety, and improved social skills rest on the foundation of his relationship with me. How can another adult move into my role when I'm out? I can't be with him every minute.

Sammy needs firm limits. A guest teacher isn't going to be comfortable setting the limits that he needs. Sammy's comfortable with those limits within the context of a close relationship with the adult who's setting them. Sammy wouldn't accept such limit setting from a stranger although he does from me.

My goal is that he behave appropriately for himself, not for me. And I do see growth. Many of his more appropriate behaviors are developing because he knows that they'll help him make friends. But he's still not ready to control himself independently. I need to remind myself that teaching is all about meeting children where they are and promoting the next stage in their growth. It's not realistic to expect that in the past six short months of the year Sammy would have reached some idealized standard of behavior. Recognizing where he actually is now, I can help him take a step forward.

A problem-solving conference: How to have a good day with a guest teacher

The next morning I invite Sammy to have lunch with me. This has become a familiar routine for us, one that we both welcome.

At lunchtime we sit down together in the classroom. "Sammy," I say, "I've seen you improve so much in your ability to control yourself. These days you sit through our entire Morning Meeting. You listen and participate. You raise your hand to speak during lessons. You listen to your work partners in small-group work."

Sammy is smiling. He knows what I'm saying is true. He's aware that he's worked hard to get here.

"I have noticed some things that I'm concerned about," I continue. "When I'm not here you say 'No' to other adults. I hear that when Ms. Greene was here, you crawled under the furniture, made noises during lessons, and said 'You aren't my teacher' to her when she told you to do something. Also you said 'No' to Ms. Jones when she told you to give her your puppet. What's going on for you when we have a guest teacher?" I ask.

"It was my Thomas Jefferson puppet," Sammy defends himself. "And Ms. Greene doesn't talk to us the way you do."

"So you didn't want to give up your puppet, and you don't like the way Ms. Greene talks. But sometimes I have to be out, and everybody deserves a day of learning when I'm out. We all created our rules so that everyone could learn. Look at our rules, Sammy. Which one might help you when we have a guest teacher?"

Sammy looks up at the rules. "Well … , actually," he says, "I think all three. If I had respected and cared for everyone, it would have been a better day. I'm supposed to listen but I said 'No' to Ms. Greene and Ms. Jones. And I didn't take care of the environment when I didn't clean up the art shelf after I made my puppet." Referring to student-created rules, so clear-cut and objective, often helps children break out of a defensive stance. Also, Sammy may get out of control sometimes, but he is consistently honest.

"I like to be here in the classroom with you, but sometimes I need to be out," I say. "When I'm out, we'll have a guest teacher. We need a plan so that you and your classmates can have a day of learning when I'm out. What might we do to fix this problem?"

"You could make sure that we always get Ms. Angelotti for our guest teacher," Sammy suggests. Ms. Angelotti student-taught with me last year, and this year she's working as a substitute teacher while she looks for a permanent teaching job. The children enjoy having Ms. Angelotti as their guest teacher. She knows how we do things and thus is able to keep the classroom routines consistent.

I write Sammy's idea down: "Ask Ms. Angelotti." I know we can't always request specific guest teachers, but at this stage we're brainstorming ideas, not evaluating their feasibility, so I write down all ideas. We'll both wait to comment on them once we have a list.

"What if I went to Ms. White's room?" Sammy asks. "She knows me, and I think I could have a good day in her class." Ms. White is my across-the-hall third grade teaching partner. We often teach small groups of each other's students, so she knows all the third graders well. Sammy may be on to something here. Perhaps Ms. White and I could work out a swap. Just last week one of her students put his head down on his desk, wailed loudly, and refused to participate when her class had a guest teacher. Maybe I could take Jerome whenever Ms. White is out, and she could take Sammy when I'm out.

Sammy and I continue to create our list of possibilities. I suggest that he write himself a reminder about following our rules when I'm out. He suggests that he sit next to Max when I'm out and Max can help him follow the rules.

We look at the list together. "Which of these ideas look like they might work?" I ask.

"I'm not sure that I can stay in control just because I've written myself a reminder," Sammy says. "It's hard for me to control myself, you know."

"I'm not sure we can count on Ms. Angelotti whenever I need to be out," I comment. "I do ask for her whenever I can, but some days she's busy."

"I'm not sure that Max being my partner would help all that much," Sammy admits. "After all, he sometimes helps me make my pop-ups during group lessons when you're out."

"I could ask Ms. White what she thinks about you joining her class when I'm out," I say. "We can meet again and talk about this some more after I've talked with her."

After school I discuss Sammy's idea with Ms. White. After Jerome's meltdown the previous week, she's delighted at the idea. We haven't solved the problem of the days when we both need to be out, but we have a plan for part of the problem.

The next time I'm out, Sammy joins Ms. White's class for the day. He indeed participates fully in her class, and students in both classes have a successful day.

From my journal, March 10:

My goal, in all student discipline, is to teach children skills that they can use independently. It's clear from recent events that Sammy is still highly dependent on the structures that I provide to behave calmly and preserve the learning environment for all children in our class. Nonetheless, the fact that he thought of an idea for how to maintain control when I'm not around enhances his investment in regulating his own behaviors. We've taken a step forward.

Chapter Ten

Moving toward Independent Learning

We're studying money. I read aloud to the class *Alexander, Who Used to be Rich Last Sunday* by Judith Viorst. We play with the money amounts. "What if Alexander had $5.00?" I ask.

"He could buy some sparkly colored markers for $3.99, give a dollar to his brother, and have a penny left over for himself," Sammy offers.

Leonardo the Eraser, Who Used to Be Rich Last Sunday

"You're going to write picture books today about someone who used to be rich," I tell the class. "The main character could be you, or it could be a fictional character." The children's stories, I explain to them, must have at least five money transactions. The children have to show, in equations or number sentences, how much money their character has at the beginning and end of each transaction.

The children are bubbling over with excitement. "Can we spend our money at the pet store?" asks Lori.

"Can we put money in the bank?" asks Paul.

"I'm buying fishing gear," announces Garret.

"Whatever you like, as long as your story contains five money transactions and the equations that show them," I restate.

Everyone gets to work, including Sammy. I cruise through the room, making sure each student has gotten a start on the project. Sammy has created the character of Leonardo the Eraser. *Leonardo the Eraser, Who Used to be Rich Last Sunday,* Sammy titles his piece.

"Leonardo the Eraser needs a friend. He buys a pencil to keep himself company," Sammy begins. Sammy's sentence is fluent and full of voice. He writes in cursive, using paper with widely spaced lines and a clear red midline to keep his lower-case letters in place. "$10.00 - $.79 = $9.21." He includes the required math information.

Leonardo buys school supplies to keep himself company and gives money away to his eraser brothers, named Leonardo II and Leonardo III. Starting with the template of Judith Viorst's already created story, Sammy is able to plug in his own character and use his unique sense of humor to enliven the story.

"Sammy," I say, "you're approaching this assignment efficiently." There was a time, not so long ago, when Sammy would have cut out scores of fake paper dollar bills and spread them out over the floor, forgetting the purpose of the assignment in his flurry of paper.

"I notice how legible your cursive writing is," I add. "I can understand everything you've written." After months of practicing cursive writing in his cursive workbook, Sammy has taken a leap and is now able to write legible cursive letters automatically so that he can form his letters and compose his ideas simultaneously.

What progress he's made!

Bubbles the Fish, glug, glug, glug

State testing is approaching, and the children are practicing writing short, focused pieces similar to the ones they'll need to write for the test. I give them big pieces of chart paper, partner them up, and have each partnership spend a half hour writing a story together. Partners read their stories aloud, and then the whole class scores the stories, using anchor sets provided by the state. Their scoring is accurate. Because of the sense of community in our classroom, built up over months, the partner-work aspect makes this test prep low-risk and fun.

The next day we do individual test practice. Sammy writes a story about Bubbles the Fish. Bubbles—"glug, glug, glug"—is swimming in a river when he gets caught by Paul. Paul takes Bubbles home and makes friends with him.

When the half-hour writing period is over, Sammy shows his story to Paul. "Look, Paul, I wrote about you fishing," he announces proudly. Paul grins broadly.

From my journal, March 15:

The concept of efficiency is taking hold. Sammy wrote his Leonardo the Eraser money story with organization and voice. His Bubbles the Fish story was focused and funny. Sammy needs clear limits for his behavior. He also needs clear limits for his academic work. Modeling, coaching, reinforcements, reminders, redirections, the RSC place, and other structures for stopping misbehavior help Sammy meet basic classroom expectations. With templates to follow and reminders about efficiency, his writing is becoming organized, clear, and elaborated. It's still brief and often labored, but the growth is remarkable.

"I have ADD, you know."

The children are working in pairs, listening to each other's writing. Sammy is listening to Paul's story about a fishing trip with his grandfather. "Could you read that again?" Sammy asks. "I have ADD, you know." Paul rereads the paragraph and this time Sammy attends.

The teachers who work with Sammy recently completed a set of rating scales, analyzing Sammy's school behaviors in order to help us think about whether some of his challenges might be related to ADD. After sharing the results with his parents, the school psychologist met with Sammy to explain the findings. I have noticed that it's often helpful for children who are eight, nine, and older to understand their learning challenges as identified by the adults in their lives. That way they can be active participants in using the strategies that have been determined could help them learn. Sammy asking Paul to reread is an example of this. Michele, who also is being looked at for ADD, takes a brisk walk down the hall before it's time to pay attention in a whole-group lesson.

Sometimes, though, Sammy uses his identification as a person with ADD to blame those around him for interpersonal bumps in the road. Walking away from a talk with Michele about whether he helped clean up their work area, Sammy mumbles, "They just pick on me because I have ADD." It may be true that it's hard for him to focus on cleaning up. But Michele's concern was Sammy's behavior, because it's hard for her to do her work when the table is strewn with pop-ups. I often find myself privately saying to Sammy things like "It's not because you have ADD, Sammy. Remember when Michele told you that she couldn't do her work with your pop-ups spread out all over the table? She just needs space to do her work." My job is to help Sammy see his ADD as what it is (a learning challenge) and what it isn't (a weakness that other children use against him).

My role as teacher to all of the children

It's Tuesday morning at 10:00, math time. The children have made choices about how they might best practice their fraction skills. I watch the students at work. Paul and Halima are playing Concentration, matching fraction picture cards with their numerical fraction representations. Robert and Patricia are writing fraction story problems for Chris and Michele to solve, while Chris and Michele write fraction story problems for Robert and Patricia. Jerry, Paulina, Juan, and Max are playing Cover Up with their sets of student-made fraction bar kits and a die.

Sammy is working by himself. He has a set of twelve beads and is dividing them into as many different fractional parts as he can, drawing simple pictures and labeling the pictures. First he creates equal groups. Two groups of six beads each means that six out of twelve beads = 1/2 of the beads. Three groups of four beads each mean that four out of twelve beads = 1/3 of the beads. He's not the only student working by himself. Lori, Mitsuke, Sofia, and Lexi have also chosen to work alone.

Sammy's made a good choice. Despite the fact that I've been working with him on social skills for the past seven months, he still needs support to work smoothly with classmates. For this math choice period, the goal is to practice fractions. He can do that better without the added demands of social interaction.

Making appropriate learning choices and implementing them like this does not come naturally for most children. The teacher has to teach the skills for independent work and provide a structure that engenders success. For this math choice period, I made sure the whole class understood the learning goals, and I limited their choices of activity to ones that will facilitate meeting the goals. We learned about handling the math materials safely and carefully and explored their potential uses. As a class, we've reflected on how to know which skills we need to improve and which activities might offer that skill work. The children have practiced under my guidance. Their independence now is based on carefully scaffolded skill instruction.

How does a student like Sammy influence a class's ability to have this kind of learning experience? In the beginning of the year, when Sammy's tantrums disrupted lessons, such peaceful learning would have been out of the question. But in a way, Sammy—or my work with Sammy—has been good for us all. I've used social skills instruction (both whole-group and individual), redirections, the RSC place, problem-solving conferences, and more to help Sammy get himself under control. This teaching has benefited Sammy, but it's also benefited the whole class, providing a safe and calm learning environment for all.

It works the other way around, too. Without an atmosphere of predictability for the entire class, the strategies that I've used with Sammy would have been far less effective. He has needed the firm foundation of safety, kindness, and calm in order to learn new social skills. Without this environment, my efforts to help Sammy would have been like paddling upstream through rough waters, our small boat getting tossed over with every wave. By helping Sammy I've helped the entire class. By helping the entire class I've helped Sammy.

PART 4

THE END OF THE YEAR

April through June

The Totem Pole Project

It's April. The students have grown. Their physical growth is most apparent, but I'm struck by their emotional and social growth as well. "Can we invite our first grade buddies to play outdoor games with us?" asks Chris. Only a few months ago he was so intent on playing himself that he was barely able to pay attention to his first grade buddy. Meanwhile, some of the girls are starting to picture themselves "liking" boys. "Have you ever kissed Alex?" asks a note crumpled up on the floor between Sofia and Pua.

Our community is strong. "I found a book in the library that I think Sammy will like," announces Paul. "Zoe, will you help me with my spelling words?" requests Jenny. "Do you have someone to eat lunch with?" Michele asks Halima. More and more I notice the children actively listening to each other, volunteering to help each other out, befriending a student who is alone.

It's a good time for an extended collaborative project. This winter the class learned about the Native Americans of the Eastern Woodlands. That study was done with a lot of direct instruction and supervision by me. Now the class is ready to learn about a similar topic more independently, working in teams to study Native Americans from another part of the continent. This is part of a third-grade-wide project in which each class will investigate a different geographical region. The common curricular focus will be the relationship between geography and culture—how the Native Americans of each region adapted to their environment. The children will do research, and then each class will create a museum to teach the other third grade classes what they learned.

Our class will be studying the Native Americans of the Pacific Northwest. Each small group will investigate one aspect of the culture of Native Americans from this region.

Initial forays into the subject

To launch the unit, I gather the children for a story. They sit on the floor, comfortably clumped, while I tell a folk tale about Raven, an important figure in many Pacific Northwest cultures. After the tale, I say, "We're going to study about the people who first told the Raven stories. What are you wondering about the Native Americans of the Pacific Northwest?"

The children's questions are informed by our Eastern Woodlands study. "What did they eat?" "Did they hunt?" "Did they plant?" "What did they wear?" "What were their houses like?" "What did the kids play?" I record their questions on large chart paper. Over the next few days, our class studies the abundant habitat of the Pacific Northwest and begins to learn about the people who lived there. Some children listen to folk tales and recorded music; others study photos of artifacts; some search websites. We add to our collective list of questions.

Once the children have a beginning knowledge base, it's time to choose their area of concentration.

"I want to study totem poles because they're like my pop-ups."

Based on the children's questions about Pacific Northwest peoples and the essential curricular question of the relationship between geography and culture, I've prepared a list of possible topics of concentration. After seeing the list, the students are to write me a letter explaining what they want to study and why.

"I want to study totem poles because they're like my pop-ups," Sammy writes. "Also, I know that they have something to do with animals and I am very interested in animals."

I decide to grant Sammy's request because he's passionate about his interests and I'd like to build on that passion. Working with a group won't be easy for him. By assigning him a topic that he cares deeply about, I'm adding to his chances of success.

Moreover, Marie's first choice is also totem poles. If they're in the same group, Marie's paraprofessional will be able to help keep Sammy on track. Sammy's grown a lot, but I don't think he's ready to work with peers for long stretches of time without close adult supervision. Plus, Max has listed totem poles as his first choice, as has Jerry. Max and Jerry are both responsible workers. They'll anchor the group, and Sammy will be delighted to get to work with Max.

What skills will the children need?

For the next month the children will work fairly independently in groups of three or four. I'll give all of the groups structure and support along the way, but this project is still a big step up from the passion study where they worked alone and didn't need to get along with anybody. It's also a big step from reading and writing conferences where they have to collaborate with only one person. I spend some time thinking, "What skills will the students need?" I list the following:

- Taking turns speaking

- Listening and responding to each other's ideas

- Making decisions that feel comfortable to everyone in the group

I break it down further:

- What are the skills involved in taking turns speaking? The children will need to decide who speaks first, second, and third. They haven't had a lot of experience doing this type of turn-taking in a group of more than two. I decide to do a whole-class role-play of this skill.

- Listening and responding to someone else's ideas is something these students have practiced a lot in Morning Meeting, so I think I can just remind them about it. Sammy may need some extra reminders and reinforcements for this one as it's an area he continues to struggle with.

- Making decisions based on everyone's ideas involves compromising. We've practiced that as part of class problem-solving meetings, but it's something I'll need to remind the children to do as well. Sammy may need some one-on-one coaching on this type of compromise. I'll watch and see.

Browse, read, report

Yesterday the class role-played ways to take turns speaking in their groups. They tried using a talking stick and having a group leader who calls on people. They role-played taking turns being group leader if more than one person wanted that job. The class agreed that these would be their methods for making sure everyone in their groups gets an equal chance to speak.

With that, the children are ready for today's activity, which will require turn-taking with group mates. During literacy block, they'll read about their chosen topics and then share what they learned with their group. I've gathered books from the local library, thinking of specific children as I collected. There are a couple of easy-to-read books about plank houses for Michele, Jenny, and Garret. There's a book about food-gathering practices with complex sentences, implied meanings, and challenging vocabulary for Robert.

"Today you'll read to learn," I explain. "Your job is to browse through your group's stack of books and choose one that seems right for you. Once you've chosen your book, you'll read for twenty minutes and then tell your group what you learned. Before you tell about your learning, be sure to decide together which method you'll use to determine who will speak first."

I post an agenda for reading time:

10:00–10:15	Browse
10:15–10:35	Read one book
10:35–10:40	Decide about turn-taking
10:40–11:00	Report on reading

Right now, while the children are learning how to work with a group, they need lots of explicit instruction.

As they begin to read, I say to Sammy, "Remember, listen to Marie, Max, and Jerry."

The children are focused. Glancing around the room, I see Jenny, Michele, and Garret excitedly pointing to diagrams showing the construction of plank houses. I see Sofia reading about clothing made of tree bark. I see Paul and Mitsuke partner reading about the life cycle of the salmon. Marie's paraprofessional, Ms. Jones, is prompting Marie with an index card that says, "Browse, choose a book." Sammy is absorbed in a thick, complex book about specific totem poles and how they reflect the culture of the people who made them.

As the children read, I circulate and check in. Manuel reads a short selection aloud to me. Sofia tells me the most important thing she's learned so far. I'm attending to fluency, checking comprehension.

When the children begin telling each other what they learned in their reading, I listen with a different ear. Are they sharing important information or merely reciting everything they read? Are they taking turns? Asking each other questions?

I join the totem pole group, knowing this is the part of the agenda that would be most challenging for Sammy. Sammy is reading aloud from his book, complicated and full of dense vocabulary. "Read slowly so that I can understand," requests Marie. "Marie has certainly grown socially," I think to myself.

Meanwhile, however, Sammy crawls under the table and makes a high-pitched whining sound, like metal against metal in an oil-less engine. I look at him and subtly give him the sign language R-for-reminder. He glares at me, saying, "They're just doing it to annoy me. Even my baby cousin understands when I read to him."

I separate Sammy from the group. "Sammy, take a deep breath and go get a drink of water. Then we'll talk." When he returns, I say, "Sammy, your baby cousin would listen to you whether he understands you or not. Your group needs to understand you in order to get their work done. What can you do to help your group and be a participating member?"

Sammy, calmer now, replies, "I could go back and read slowly." He returns to his group and quietly joins them. First he listens to Jerry tell about his selection. Then he takes his turn, slowly and clearly reading one important sentence aloud. I give him a private, nonverbal thumbs up.

From my journal, April 11:

In my preparation for this project I analyzed the tasks that would be challenging for the group and for Sammy in particular. I explicitly taught needed skills, put structures in place to maximize Sammy's chances of success, and gave him extra reminders. Although Sammy and I have been able to reduce the number and severity of his meltdowns, we haven't been able to prevent them completely, as much as I wish we could have. Sammy still gets annoyed when other children express their desires. He thinks they're purposefully irritating him and loses control in his annoyance.

However, it's now possible for me to bring Sammy back. Today he was already working himself into a spiral of high-pitched whining, and yet it was possible to separate him from the group and, after he'd taken a couple of deep breaths and a drink of water, even reason with him. Not only did he regain enough control to be open to reason, but he then was able to rejoin the group and make amends by listening and contributing.

Days pass. The children have been reading about their topics. They've raised and discussed questions. They've written down important information. They've thought about how the information they've gleaned relates to our essential question, "How did the Native Americans of the Pacific

Northwest adapt in order to survive and prosper in their environment?" It's time for each group to pick a project that will show their answer to this question.

Picking a project: What might be fun? What might be hard?

"Today you're going to start discussing with your group how to show your learning about how the Native Americans of the Pacific Northwest adapted in order to survive and prosper in their environment," I write in the morning message. "What will be fun about this? What will be hard?" Responses to the "fun" question include "Being creative" and "Making things." Responses on the "hard" side include "Agreeing" and "Arguments."

As we go over the morning message, I bring up the issue of compromising. "We've practiced compromising in lots of situations," I remind the class. "When have we compromised?"

The children share many examples. "Yesterday Michele and Patricia wanted to jump rope and I wanted to play Four Square. We compromised and jumped rope for a while. Then we switched to Four Square," says Jenny. "We compromised about what to play when our first grade buddies joined us for outdoor games," says Juan. "We had to think about which games we like, which ones we thought our buddies would like, and then choose just a few."

Confident that most of the children remember what it means to compromise, I send them off to brainstorm potential projects with their groups. The children happily make long lists of ideas. The clothing group, for example, thinking about how rain-shedding hats and bark capes helped the native people survive in their rainy environment, discuss drawing posters, creating costumes for themselves, bringing in dolls from home, and making doll clothes.

I know that the totem pole group is going to need extra supervision with this socially and emotionally demanding step. Ms. Jones is out sick today, so they don't have her support. I'm going to need to encourage Marie to assert herself and Sammy to listen to others. "Remember, Sammy, listen to your group mates," I whisper to him as the children head off to work.

Later, I listen in. "Let's make pop-ups of totem poles," suggests Sammy. Jerry, the group recorder, writes down "Pop-ups."

"We could make 3-D totem poles using empty tissue rolls," suggests Max.

Marie is humming to herself and playing with her fingers. I sit next to her and hold up an index card that says, "Project ideas." Marie looks around and says, "Draw pictures." Jerry writes that down.

Just then, Halima, from the clothing group, comes over and politely interrupts to ask me what materials are available to her group. I leave the totem pole group to join the clothing group. Such is classroom life. Teachers need to attend to all students' needs and can't always stay with the children with challenges as much as would be ideal. With the clothing group, I discuss paper, paint, and some donated fabric in the third grade closet. Meanwhile, I hear ever-increasing volume from the totem pole corner. I look across the room to see Sammy slumped in his chair, slowly sliding into his safe place under the table. I rejoin his group and give Sammy his nonverbal R-for-reminder. This time he pulls himself together and sits up. 'What's going on?" I ask.

"Sammy wants our project to be a pop-up, and the rest of us want to make 3-D models with tissue rolls," explains Max.

"I don't like tissue rolls," explains Sammy. "I think they're gross." I'm mentally celebrating the fact that, at least in this moment, he's expressing his opinion forthrightly and at least somewhat respectfully.

"I have an idea," says Jerry. "When I was in first grade my third grade buddy was in this class and he was in the totem pole group. They made huge totem poles out of giant cardboard rolls. They went all the way up to the ceiling."

The group is electrified. All four are talking at once, asking me, "Can we do that? Can we do that?"

"Sure," I reply. "I still have the giant cardboard rolls. They're in the third grade closet."

From my journal, April 20:

Jerry saved the day by bringing in another possibility, one that no eight-year-old could resist. They all love projects that are big. His suggestion effectively released everyone from having to do the hard work of compromising. Still, it demonstrated sophisticated problem-solving. I'm struck by how skillfully children are able to negotiate sticky situations involving Sammy. The world is filled with all kinds of people, and students learn valuable life lessons from working with children who present interpersonal challenges.

Sammy is improving. A nonverbal reminder, delivered before he was fully out of control, got him back on track. So his R-for-reminder idea is working after all, at least when he's not too far gone. He resumed sharing his concerns and listening to group mates' ideas and was even ready to give up his idea once a very attractive alternative was raised. Earlier in the year he wouldn't have considered even the most appealing of ideas if they weren't his.

Nonetheless, Sammy just doesn't have the level of social maturity that most of his classmates have. The Native American project, independent, long term, necessitating group collaboration and compromise, is perfect for most of the students, who are developmentally eight and nine. It's far more challenging for Sammy. I'm raising the bar with this project. Sammy's going to need continued support from me in order to reach it.

Hiding in a locker to seek solace

The Native American project is a special opportunity for family involvement. Children are painting, cutting, and sewing. The tools group is even doing simple carving. Especially for these messier or potentially dangerous crafts, I need help with supervision. For family and friends who are able to, getting involved in such project-oriented learning is a way to gain some perspective on what their child's school day is like.

On this Tuesday afternoon, the room is buzzing with activity. Garret's grandmother is helping Jenny, Michele, and Garret figure out how to make the roof of their plank house model lift off so people can see inside. Paul and Mitsuke are working independently on a large poster about the life cycle of the salmon. Halima's mother, able to join us because she's been out of work for the past few months, is threading needles so that Halima, Sofia, Chris, and Alex can sew the costumes they're creating out of fabric from the third grade closet and bark they found on the playground. For once, I'm pleased that I save everything that might come in handy someday.

The totem pole group has planned their totem poles, sketched the paintings on brown butcher paper, cut the paper to fit around the large cardboard tubes, and laid out the paper in our wide hall. Sammy's mom, Mrs. Smith, has volunteered to spend her afternoon off from work supervising the potentially messy task of painting the animal drawings with poster paint.

Before they begin, I remind the group about safe and careful use of the paint. We review what to do with wet paint brushes and the importance of keeping everything on the newspapers protecting the floor under their painting. Checking in on the group later, I see Jerry, Max, Sammy, and Marie all painting their animals. As they work, they chat companionably about the animals and what they've learned about Native Americans, as well as a children's movie that Sammy and Jerry both saw on TV. "What do you call a Roman emperor with a cold?" Sammy asks Jerry. "I don't know. What?" "Julius Sneezer." They giggle happily. I go into the classroom to check on the other groups.

When I return to the hall to see how the totem pole group is doing, Max and Jerry are staring at the lockers. Marie is happily painting away. Mrs. Smith is standing in the middle of the hall looking nonplussed, and Sammy is missing. "Where's Sammy?" I ask.

"He's in the locker," explains Max. There he is, crammed into an upper level locker, with the door partially closed.

"Sammy, if you need to regain self-control, you need to do so in our room, not in a locker," I say calmly.

"I'm staying here," he announces gruffly.

If Sammy doesn't want to get down out of the locker, I can't force him to. I need some back up. "Max, will you please go get Ms. White?" I ask. Max goes to get my third grade teaching neighbor. Since the fall, I've rehearsed this "buddy teacher" routine with the class for just these instances when I need a colleague's help. As Ms. White leaves her room, I go to stand in her doorway to supervise her class. "Sammy's in an upper level locker," I whisper to her as she walks past.

Ms. White walks up to the locker and quietly says, "Sammy, come with me." With a new adult in the picture, the tension is broken and Sammy clambers down. He follows Ms. White across the hall to sit in her class's "take a break" chair.

I return to the totem pole group and ask, "What happened?"

"Sammy didn't want me to paint my frog green," explained Manuel. "He said that it was a toad and ought to be brown."

As the group returns to painting, I quietly discuss the events with Mrs. Smith. "They were all getting along so well at first," she reports. "Then Sammy started to argue with Max and Jerry about every little thing: the colors they were using, how well they were keeping the paint in the lines, where they were sitting. He wanted me to take his side and insist that they do things his way. I tried to help them reach agreement, but since I wasn't taking his side, he got more and more upset until he finally crawled into the locker."

"Sometimes it's hard to share your mom with other kids," I sympathize.

The students clean up their projects, put them away for safekeeping, and line up for PE. I go to collect Sammy.

From my journal, April 25:

Sammy's behavior today reminds me of when my own daughter was in preschool. I was so excited the day I got to go to her school and help out. To my surprise, she hung onto my leg and screamed the whole time,

"My mommy, my mommy!" fending off any other children who might try to interact with me. Sammy's so mature intellectually, yet he's like a younger child in certain ways. Apparently, this is one of those ways. He wanted his mom to help him get his way in even the smallest decisions about the project. I'm not sorry that Mrs. Smith joined us today. I hope she'll be able to join us again. Next time I'll anticipate Sammy's behavior and prep him in advance.

As for Sammy's hiding in a locker, crawling into an upper level and trying to close the locker door isn't safe. On the other hand, Sammy was giving himself a kind of RSC, finding a private place where he could seek solace. In his own way, he's learning to manage his emotions.

The big day

It's the big day, the day of our museum. The children have created their displays. They've prepared and practiced presentations that explain their information. We have our schedule for when the classes will visit each other's museums.

The totem poles are built, and Sammy's group has carefully planned a system that allows each member an equal chance to speak. As Jerry begins, Sammy listens. "The Native Americans of the Pacific Northwest lived in an abundant environment. Food was readily available, and the weather was mild." Sammy takes his turn on cue: "As a result, they had plenty of time to make up stories and carve totem poles. Each totem pole tells a story." Next it's Max's turn. "We have made up a story to go with our totem pole. Once upon a time, raven was hungry." Marie continues the story. Sammy's moving, hopping on one foot, but he's still listening, ready for his next cue.

From my journal, April 29:

Sammy did it. It wasn't easy—this kind of group collaboration pushes the limits of his readiness—but he gave it a good effort, and he succeeded. The more I was able to predict what might be tough for him and give him coaching ahead of time, the more successful he was. It's easy to have moments of thinking, "Why am I still giving him this kind of coaching when it's nearly May?" But then I remind myself, "I've raised the bar a lot here. I'm expecting more, and it's quite an achievement that he's meeting this new standard, albeit with some help."

Chapter Twelve

Celebrating Growth at Parent-Student-Teacher Conferences

Spring parent conferences are coming up. In my classes, the students are present at the spring conferences, making them three-way parent-student-teacher conversations. In fact, the students lead these meetings—by presenting samples of their work that show their learning during the past months and talking about the samples with their families.

To prepare for the conferences, the children will have to reflect on the question, *How did I grow this past quarter?* Reflection isn't new to these children. All year long we've been reflecting on our behavior and learning. *How did we do at walking down the hall quietly today so as not to disturb the other classes? What did we do this week that follows our rule "Be kind"? Which book is right for you? Which strategy did you use to solve the math problem? What question did your partner ask you that helped you improve your writing?* These questions fill our days. The next logical step is for the children to reflect globally on their learning.

Which papers show my growth in math?

We begin by focusing on our math learning. The children's math folders are stuffed with papers from February, March, and April. Today they'll peruse these papers to find evidence of their math learning this quarter.

I model first. I leaf through Zoe's folder, reading each paper. I comment on some, pretending to be the student. "Hmmm, this one is an example of how much more I know about multiplication now. I used to only know my twos. Now I know all my facts through five." I ask the students what they noticed.

"You read every paper," says Chris.

"You picked a paper from a while ago—only knowing the twos— to show what you learned," adds Mitsuke.

Next I ask for a student volunteer. Juan leafs through the papers at the front of his math folder, the ones from February. He picks out a paper from our geometry study and says, "I learned so much when we studied geometry. I didn't even know what a polygon was before that."

"What did you notice about what Juan did with his math papers?" I ask the class.

"He thought about how much he learned back when we studied geometry," Patricia volunteers.

"He looked at them carefully," adds Garret.

"So," I say, "you're each going to go through your math folders and think about your work. Take your time. Choose at least three papers that show something you're proud of learning this quarter. Then take an index card and write on it, 'This piece shows my learning because …' I'll be watching you as you reflect on your math learning."

This is not a new task. The children prepared portfolios before fall parent-teacher conferences and before January report cards. This task was frustrating for Sammy then, and I suspect it's going to be tough for him this time around as well. Organization is one of his challenges. A folder full of three months of math papers is going to feel overwhelming to him.

I sit next to Sammy and watch as he rapidly leafs through his papers. "Remind me what Juan and I showed the class when we modeled looking at math papers," I say.

"You thought about what you learned," he replies.

"What did we do first to allow us to think about that?"

"You read some papers. I guess I'd better do that."

Sammy reads through some papers. He finds a problem-solving paper where he made a table to show his thinking. Taking an index card, he writes, "This paper shows my learning because I learned to make a table to show my thinking." He staples the index card to his paper and continues to examine his papers. "Well," I muse silently as I move on to help another student, "despite an iffy start, he did fine with some individual coaching. It helps that the coaching came early, and that he has math papers he's genuinely proud of."

What about the empty reader's notebook?

The next day, the students pick samples of their reading work to share at their conferences. Their goal is to choose a book they've read that shows how they've grown as readers and a notebook entry that shows how they think as readers.

Sammy is proud of the fact that he's branched out as a reader and has read some challenging historical fiction. "I loved *Sign of the Beaver*. I understood it and it was about history," he writes on a sticky note that he affixes to the cover of the book.

Picking a reader's notebook entry is another matter. The sad fact is that Sammy's notebook is empty. There are a few dates and scrawled beginnings of book titles, but not a single real entry. Sammy crawls on the floor and meows like a cat, bothering his classmates. It looks to me like he's frustrated. "What's going on?" I ask him.

"I hate my reader's notebook."

"I can see that you don't have any entries," I reply neutrally. "What are you going to tell your family at your conference?" Sammy had gotten back into his seat, but now starts to slide down his chair, moving toward his hiding place under his table. "How about making writing in your notebook a goal?" I suggest. Part of the conference is devoted to setting goals for the remainder of the year.

"I can't. I don't have anything to say," is his immediate response.

"I can help you."

"OK," he agrees, and sits up a little straighter. He has grown since September. He wouldn't have agreed to such a suggestion in the fall or even in January. But now he's willing to at least think about trying.

Rehearsals for the upcoming meetings

The family meetings are right around the corner. Each student presents his portfolio to me as a rehearsal for the upcoming event. I hear about multiplication facts learned and others targeted to be learned. "I can solve hard problems like this one," says Patricia, showing me her math paper. I hear about growth in reading fluency and accuracy. I hear about improvement in writing. "Now my writing has lots of details," explains Max. I add information that I've noticed about each child's academic growth.

I also ask the children about work habits and social skills. "Who do you work and play with?" In contrast to when we prepped for November conferences, now many children mention that they enjoy working and playing with Sammy. This is surely a sign that Sammy's becoming more flexible in the give and take of friendship. It's also a sign that his classmates have gained more skills in getting along with someone who's a little different. They've learned to appreciate him for his interesting ideas and sense of humor, while he's learned to behave more respectfully toward them.

When it's Sammy turn to rehearse, he displays a sheaf of successful math papers. "I'm good at math," he says. He proudly shows me some brief but well organized and elaborated pieces of writing. "Cursive writing helps me," he explains. "And now I can write a story that is easy to understand and funny." He shows me *Leonardo the Eraser, Who Used to Be Rich Last Sunday* and says, "The kids laughed when I read this to the class."

"It helps when you have a format to follow," I comment.

Then I bring up the topic of friendships. "How are things going with friends?" I ask.

"Max was in my Native American group," he replies. "That was fun."

Seeing my opportunity to help Sammy recognize and enjoy other friendships, I say, "I've noticed that you have some other friends, too. You and Michele have fun going on errands together. You play with a lot of classmates at recess now, especially Paul. You wrote your *Bubbles the Fish* story about Paul."

"But if Max would only play with me at recess," Sammy continues.

"I can see that you feel that way," I say, "but Max likes to play football, and you prefer to play tag. We each have our own interests."

"Sammy," I go on, "your friends are the people who work with you and play with you, who laugh with you and want to be with you. That would describe both Michele and Paul as well as some other kids." Sammy listens but has a skeptical look on his face.

We move on to another topic for now. Together, Sammy and I list goals for the rest of the year. "Learn math," he writes. He looks at me and explains, "I'm good at math, but I know there are going to be new things to learn in the next two months." Then he writes, "Read more books."

"What about your reader's notebook?" I ask.

Without missing a beat, he says, "Yup, I need one about that." He writes, "Write in my reader's notebook."

I ask, "Do you want to set a goal that names a number of sentences?" I'm asking—if he says no, I'd accept that. I help, encourage, and nudge, but ultimately these need to be his goals.

"Two sentences for an entry," he adds. I accept that as a realistic goal.

"Write at writing time," he lists.

"I think you're ready to present your portfolio to your family," I tell him.

Conference day: Sammy presents with poise and clarity

On the day of his conference, Sammy sits next to me, his mother and father facing us across the table. He confidently explains his growth in math, reading, and writing. The adults all smile with delight. He next shares his goal of writing two sentences per entry in his reader's notebook and writing at writing time.

Then Mrs. Smith turns to the social issues. "How are things going with friends?" she asks.

"I like to work and play with lots of kids," Sammy says. "I cooperated during the Native American project," he continues. "But I still wish that Max was my best friend."

Mrs. Smith is getting that familiar look of concern on her face. I need to inject another perspective into the discussion. "Sammy, Max enjoyed working with you on the Native American project," I say. "He has lots of friends. Maybe he prefers to have lots of friends rather than one best friend."

From my journal, May 1:

Sammy presented his portfolio with poise and clarity. It was striking to see how much he's grown academically.

I'm also thinking about the way many students reported enjoying working and playing with Sammy. He has so many strengths. He's smart, funny, and charming, and his classmates obviously like these qualities in him. This is an example of an important strength of our community— that everyone has a chance to get to know everyone else well, and everyone comes to appreciate each other despite behaviors that can be annoying in the moment. One of the things I love about teaching is this opportunity to help children see that everyone is worthy.

Sammy's desire for one close friend continues to be an issue. He's intense. It's hard to picture one student being able to handle that intensity all the time. Also, our class is a strong community and the children are, for the most part, friendly to everyone. Best friend dyads are infrequent in our group, and most children have a variety of people that they like to work and play with. If I can help Sammy reflect on this fact, he'll be less likely to hem Max in, reducing the possibility that Max might avoid or even reject him. I know that Sammy heard my words, but did he believe me? Time will tell.

Book Clubs

You worked cooperatively with your Native American groups," I tell the class. "I can see that you're ready for book clubs. You're nearly ready for fourth grade."

These students have noticed the fourth graders sitting out in the hall engaged in their book clubs, a student leader facilitating the discussions. It's something they're all looking forward to next year. Doing book clubs now at the end of third grade will allow them to consolidate the literacy and collaboration skills they've been learning all year and build confidence for the grade ahead.

"I'm going to suggest some books for you to choose among," I continue. "You'll say which book you want to read and discuss. I'll form groups from your book choices."

For starters, I've picked out rich picture books for them to select from. All are short texts with thought-provoking settings and issues that will trigger discussion. The children will select based on interest and meet once or twice in a group for each book. After they've learned to conduct book clubs with these short-term groups, we'll move on to chapter books.

Unlike our guided reading groups, which are organized by reading level, these groups will each include a mix of reading abilities. To make such multi-level groups possible, children will have the option of reading the book themselves or asking a parent, sibling, or friend to read it to them.

Choosing books

I unveil the books. *My Rotten Redheaded Older Brother* is a tale of sibling rivalry and love by Patricia Polacco. *Sweet Clara and the Freedom Quilt* by Deborah Hopkinson is set in the days of slavery and tells how a girl helps others escape. *The Day of Ahmed's Secret* by Florence Parry Heide and Judith Heide Gilliland, and illustrated by Ted Lewin, tells about a working boy in Cairo whose secret is that he's learned to write his name. *Baseball Saved Us* by Ken Mochizuki and illustrator Dom Lee, set in a U.S. Japanese-American internment camp during World War II, tells about how playing baseball strengthened the internees' community and kept them working together.

The children are excited. I notice that Frankie, who often has tussles with his brother, chooses *My Rotten Redheaded Older Brother*. *Sweet Clara* is popular with many of the girls. I think they're attracted to the title. Halima, whose father is Egyptian, chooses *The Day of Ahmed's Secret*, as do several children who are curious about Halima's family culture. Many of the children who play softball at recess select *Baseball Saved Us*. I'm going to need to find some more copies of that one.

Sammy chooses *Baseball Saved Us* because of its setting, during World War II. So many children have signed up for this one that I need to create three *Baseball Saved Us* groups. As a result, I can pick and choose whom to group Sammy with. I put him with Robert and Paul. Both of them can keep up with Sammy's higher-level thinking, so there will be fewer potential "They don't understand me" disagreements. Also, reading with Paul may give Sammy a nudge toward seeing that he and Paul are friends.

From my journal, May 4:

I'm raising the bar for the class with our end-of-year studies like these book clubs. Back in September, the children worked in partnerships. Now they're working in small groups. Until recently, reading instruction happened via guided reading groups with membership and reading materials selected by me and the group discussions led by me as well. Now I'm expecting them to read in book clubs with students leading the discussion. That's a big leap, but most students will be able to handle it.

Sammy, though, is barely keeping up with the rising expectations for maturity and organization. I could excuse him from book clubs and have him continue to read independently. This might be a better match with his current skills and abilities. On the other hand, he so wants to engage socially with the other children, and book clubs are such an important part of our community process now that it's May. Being in groups also helps him inch away from his single-minded focus on Max. Working and playing with other students who'd like to befriend him, such as Paul and Michele, will help him recognize them as friends. So I'll include him in book clubs and support his efforts with reminders, redirections, reinforcement, and coaching.

Read, then think of good discussion questions

"Your job," I explain to the students, "is to read your book or ask someone to read it to you. Once you've taken in the story, you'll write three discussion questions in preparation for your group meeting. Your questions need to be open-ended discussion questions," I continue, "because these are questions that will help you have a rich conversation."

I proceed to teach about three types of questions:

■ Factual questions have one and only one right answer.

- Open-ended discussion questions have more than one correct answer that can be supported by referring to the text.

- Opinion questions have answers that are neither right nor wrong because they ask only for the reader's opinion. These questions can't be answered by referring to the text.

For their book groups, the children are to come up with questions of the second type. We practice using the story of Jack and the Beanstalk. "What did Jack trade for the beans?" is a factual question. There's only one correct answer, that he traded his cow for the beans. "Are you afraid of giants?" is clearly opinion as only the reader can know about his own feelings. But "Did Jack make a good choice to climb the beanstalk?" has many possible answers that can be backed up by the text. One could say "No," because he could have been killed by the giant, or "Yes," because he stole a golden goose that made his family rich. These are only two of the many possible answers that could be supported by text.

Sammy is engaged. "Stealing is wrong," he says, "and if Jack hadn't climbed the beanstalk he wouldn't have stolen."

"So, you can see how this might spark a rich dialogue," I say. "I predict that your group discussions are going to be interesting. Everyone will be able to contribute."

I explain the structure of the group discussion. Each child will have a turn to ask his or her first question. Whoever is asking the question gets to call on group mates to express their thoughts. Everyone needs to respond to each question at least once. Once all the first questions have been discussed, the group will begin over again with their second questions. The class listens closely. They're ready to go.

"That wasn't an open-ended question. They didn't listen to me. They never listen to me."

Sammy's group meets the next week. Robert asks the first question. "How did baseball save them?" The responses flow. "They were all so sad and mad before they started the baseball team, like when Teddy was talking back to his father," says Sammy.

"Teddy acted like a jerk," says Paul.

"Well, they were like in prison," says Robert. "We'd act like jerks, too, if we were locked up like that."

Not all the comments relate tightly to Robert's question, but the group is discussing the book productively, so I move on to listen in on another book club.

Suddenly I notice Sammy stomping around the room, loudly muttering, "They're jerks, too. They don't care what I think. That wasn't an open-ended question. They didn't listen to me." In his anger, he reaches out and flings a can of paint brushes onto the floor.

I walk over to Sammy. "Sammy, go calm down in the RSC place. Then come back and pick up the brushes." Sammy goes to RSC but continues to fling art supplies from the RSC chair, which is placed unfortunately close to the art shelf. I approach Sammy again. "You have three choices," I say. "You may calm down and rejoin your group in a respectful way. You may calm down and work by yourself writing in your reader's notebook. Or you may leave the room and calm down in Ms. White's 'take a break' chair."

Sammy continues to fling art materials, all the while saying, "They didn't listen to me. They never listen to me. That wasn't an open-ended question."

It's been a long day today with Sammy. At writing time he stood on his head and hooted instead of conferring with Marie. During Morning Meeting he snapped at Jenny when she shared, saying "That was dumb." By this point in the day I'm ready for a break from Sammy. Sammy's behavior makes it clear that calming down in Ms. White's room is the only realistic choice, and at this point I'm glad for the respite. I quietly send Paul to get Ms. White.

"I can't help it. They make me so mad," he announces angrily as he walks out with Ms. White.

As it turned out, Sammy didn't calm down in Ms. White's room either, and she called someone in the school office to come and collect him. It was much later in the day, after he'd met with our principal, when he returned to our classroom. "I'm sorry I threw the paint brushes," he apologized.

While the students are packing up to go home, I have a short conversation with Sammy.

"What happened?" I ask.

"Paul asked 'What makes this book interesting?' That's an opinion question. We all have different opinions about why it's interesting. Paul's interested in it because it's about baseball. I'm interested because it's about World War II."

"Sammy, whether you think Paul's question is appropriate or not, you need to respond to people respectfully. Which of our rules might help you with that?"

"Respect and care for everyone," he replies.

"What might you do next time to respect and care for everyone?"

"I might say, 'Paul, I think that's an opinion question. What you do think?'"

"Those are respectful words. Just now you said that with a respectful tone, too. If I were Paul, I'd be ready to listen to you."

A moment later Sammy brings me an elaborate pop-up that he created during Quiet Time. Across the front he has written in his best cursive, "I promise to be respectful."

Sammy catches himself the second time

Sammy's group didn't finish their discussion, so they continue the next day. Before they meet, I privately point to the "I promise to be respectful" sign that Sammy made. He nods and smiles and joins his group.

From across the room I see them sitting and looking at each other with respectful and engaged expressions on their faces. As I walk by I hear Sammy ask, "Why do you think Ken Mochizuki wrote this book?" All three boys carefully read the "About the author" section to find evidence to support possible answers.

A few minutes later voices rise from Sammy's group. "The guard was not being friendly," Sammy repeats with greater and greater emphasis. When Robert starts to respond, Sammy covers his ears. I watch as Sammy gets up from the group, walks to the RSC chair, and takes some deep breaths, energetically pounding his therapy putty. A moment later he returns to his group and calmly asks Robert, "Could you show us in the text where you see a clue that the guard really is being friendly?"

I think excitedly to myself, "Yes, he did it! He caught himself this time! He pulled himself back from the brink and gave a beautifully respectful response!"

Later I check in with Sammy. "What happened that allowed you to work successfully with your group today?"

"I regained self-control," he replies.

"Sammy, you can do it. Congratulations!" I say with a big smile.

Turtles are safe in their shells

Dr. Fischer, our school psychologist, stops me in the hall. "I was at a conference yesterday and heard an idea that might help Sammy when he loses control," she tells me. "The speaker talked about helping kids by using the analogy of a turtle finding a safe place in its shell."

With Dr. Fischer's guidance, I try the idea the next day. I meet with Sammy during lunch. We sit together at the reading table, eating our lunches. "Sammy," I say, "I've been thinking about the times when you lose control. I've noticed that sometimes the RSC chair isn't enough to help you regain self-control."

"Yup," Sammy answers. "Sometimes I get really, really mad." He pauses for a minute and then adds, "Like when I got so mad at Paul." I reflect on the fact that he remembers the incident with Paul. Not very long ago he would have been so out of control that he would have forgotten everything about the incident.

"So Dr. Fischer had an idea that might help you in those times," I continue. "Turtles go into their shells to be safe. Would you like to try making a special place for yourself where you could pretend to be a turtle in its shell?"

Sammy bounces a little bit in his chair with excitement, a big smile on his face. The turtle analogy seems to make sense to him. Actually, he loves turtles, so I can understand why he wants to pretend to be one. I would have dropped the idea if it didn't resonate with him.

"Where might you go if you were going to be a turtle in its shell?" I ask.

"Well ... ," he says, "I could go right under the table here." I have to think about that one for a minute. There's something that makes me uncomfortable about misbehaving children under tables, something reminiscent of children being put in the corner with a dunce cap on. On the other hand, I remind myself, we're not talking about my putting him under the table but rather about Sammy finding himself a safe, personal place in the classroom to regain self-control. He does slide under his own table and hide there when things aren't going well, and the reading table is, by design, a little out of the way, back in a corner of the classroom and thus a good private turtle spot.

"OK," I say. "Would you like to decorate the area under the table to remind you of a turtle in its shell and of regaining self-control?"

"I think it's recess time now. I told Paul I'd play with him. I'll decorate it during Quiet Time," Sammy answers. As he goes out to recess I think about how earlier in the year, recess was for him a time of stress that he would've been happy to miss. Now he has people to play with and is eager to get out there. He skips down the hall to play outside.

At Quiet Time Sammy creates posters for the underside of the reading table. The posters look like the underside of a turtle's shell. He writes such slogans as "Relax" and "Breathe" for his special place. He tapes some strips of green paper to the edge of the table so they hang down to make a curtain. I get under the table to take a look. It is lovely in his turtle shell cave.

From picture books to novels

Robert, Paul, and Sammy have decided to stay together as a group for the next stage of book clubs: reading a chapter book together. I'm pleased that they want to keep working together but a bit apprehensive about their upcoming task of choosing a book that they all want to read. Sammy is working on being a better listener, but he certainly remains inflexible when he wants something.

As with the picture books, I've offered a small array of chapter books for students to select among. Many children are intrigued by *Junebug* by Alice Mead, a novel about a boy who lives in a high-rise housing project full of gang activity. *The Castle in the Attic* by Elizabeth Winthrop interests children who like fantasy, as the main character finds himself shrunken and living in his toy castle. *Charlotte's Web* by E.B. White, a story known to many, attracts children who are reassured by the familiar. *The Hundred Dresses* by Eleanor Estes is a classic story of mean teasing and thus intrigues children who want to think about issues of teasing, exclusion, and learning to be kind. Last but not least is *Justin and the Best Biscuits in the World* by Mildred Pitts Walter, about a youngest child who learns how to be more independent due to lessons from his grandfather, an African American cowboy. The students will choose based on interest rather than reading level, as they again have the option of reading the book themselves or asking someone to read it to them.

As Sammy heads off with Paul and Robert to discuss which chapter book they'll read, I subtly point to his "I promise to be respectful" sign perched on the reading table. Sammy smiles and nods. He's full of good intentions.

A few minutes later I hear him across the room, his voice rising insistently, "But I'm interested in African Americans in cowboy days." I'm betting that Paul and Robert want to read *Junebug*. They both had lots of questions about *Junebug* when I introduced the books.

I walk over to the group. Sammy is pounding on the floor, his voice high and insistent. "You've chosen a book, and you aren't listening to me."

"Sammy," I say, "you need to regain self-control. Do you want to use the RSC chair, or do you think the turtle place might help?"

Sammy, so enthusiastic about the turtle place only yesterday, stands in the middle of the room and looks at the reading table skeptically. "OK, I'll try it just this once." He crawls under the table and curls up into a ball.

A few minutes later, he comes out with a smile, looking refreshed as he rejoins his group. I glance their way and notice the discussion continuing. The children lean into each other, faces showing engagement and interest.

At the end of reading time, the class gathers on the rug. I ask the children whether they've chosen a book. Robert and Paul still want to read *Junebug*. Jerry, Sofia, and Michele plan to read *Justin and the Best Biscuits in the World*. "Why doesn't Sammy join us?" Michele suggests. Sammy happily agrees. Just as Jerry dissolved the recent totem pole dispute with the irresistible idea of making a giant totem pole, Michele saved this conflict with an attractive solution, one that extends a hand of friendship to Sammy, to boot.

From my journal, May 7:

Using the turtle spot to calm down was a big moment for Sammy. I don't know if the turtle spot worked so well because he created it himself, because it's safe and cozy, because it's just for him, or because of the animal analogy. In any case, it feels like a turning point. With children like Sammy, as with many students, we teachers have to try different things—even in the last or next to last month of school—and see which ones stick. I'm going to continue encouraging Sammy to use his turtle spot.

Overall, Sammy has made so much progress since the beginning of the year. Whereas once he would have been intractably out of control, not even able to remember events because of the power of the emotions overtaking him, now he has some strategies and can often regain control with small prompts from me. Whereas once he would have been blaming everyone around him, saying "Even my baby cousin can do that," now he's able (after calming down) to reflect on how he might handle a situation differently next time.

There's no question that managing emotions remains a challenge for him, especially as my expectations for the class increase. In that rising sea, he sometimes sinks under water, struggling for breath. He would probably be paddling along, comfortably afloat, if my expectations of him were the same as they were in September. Would that be better? Better for whom? We teachers are constantly faced with such tough questions that have no simple answers. Sammy so desperately wants to be part of the group, to have friends. If I were to leave him out of these crucial whole-class experiences, he might be more consistently successful, but he'd be alone, going his own way. I make the choice to include him in these challenging group projects. And so we go forward, Sammy stretching and me supporting.

Chapter Fourteen

Dear Mom, This year I

The Last Six Weeks of School

The weather is bright, warm, and sunny. Summer clothing gives us all a feeling of freedom. After more than nine months together, I feel so close to and comfortable with my students.

Everything about this time of year says "Lighten up," and yet I know I need to keep our classroom structure intact. Children need more rather than less structure as the school year ends. We all need the rituals of closure, evaluating our time together, setting goals for next year, saying farewell. In addition, many children begin to feel a bit insecure toward the end of the year because they don't know what the summer will bring. Maintaining routines, reminders, and reinforcements gives such children a foundation of security. Sammy, in particular, being a child who benefits from and grows with lots of support, will need that support to be in place right up through the last day of school.

Consistent reminders and reinforcements

We're getting ready to say farewell to our first grade buddies by playing some group games with them on the playground. It's tempting to just go out and play—we've met with them so many times already. Instead, I begin with a reminder. "Who can remind us how we treat our buddies?"

"We're there to play with them, not our third grade friends," says Paulina." Early in the year this was an issue. We'd meet with our buddies, and the third graders would primarily relate to other third graders. By now, however, the buddies have real relationships and enjoy spending time together.

"We need to be kind to them, especially if they don't know how to play a game," says Sammy. Sammy needs such reminders more than many students. It's been particularly challenging for him to be attentive to his buddy, but he's learned. Now he's showing growth as he volunteers the reminders.

Out on the playground, as we play Octopus, I notice Sammy about to push his buddy aside so he himself can race to the goal. I make eye contact and show a subtle R-for-reminder. Sammy changes course. Instead of pushing, he reaches out and takes his buddy's hand so they can run together.

Back in the classroom I name things that the children did well. "I noticed all of you helping your first grade buddies," I say. "I noticed people explaining rules, holding their buddy's hand, and helping buddies remember the boundaries."

A few minutes later, I find a private moment to say to Sammy, "You were kind to Lars when you helped him run to the goal." Sammy beams.

Field day: Buckets of water and family fun

The playground is jam-packed with stations, each featuring an engaging cooperative game. Our entire school will spend most of the day rotating class by class through these stations, with children forming different teams at each station. The ever-changing-teams approach will keep the focus on collaborative fun rather than on winners and losers. Our PE teachers have been here since 4:00 AM getting everything ready. Their preparation ensures a successful day for all.

The day is steaming hot, and the children cheer when we reach "Pass the Bucket." They'll pass a bucket of water down a row of children, first under, between a child's legs, then over the next child's head—under and over, under and over—until the bucket reaches the end of the line, where the water is dumped into a plastic wading pool, signaling for the next bucket to start down the row.

The children line up. Before they begin, I say, "Remind us how we pass the bucket."

"Keep the water in the bucket," says Manuel.

"It's OK to get yourself wet, but no slopping the bucket on someone else unless they ask you, right?" asks Sammy. He's not sure. "Yes, right," I say.

"I think that getting a little wet is part of the fun," says Patricia.

"Sure," I say, "as long as you don't get soaked or get water on someone who doesn't ask for it."

The children begin. They spill the water, get wet, laugh, but keep it under control.

"It took some effort to have fun, cool down, but keep it in check," I say, reinforcing their positive behavior as we walk to the next station.

Stopping to observe

Field day is a family fun day for us. Parents, grandparents, siblings, and neighbors are invited to stop by to watch a game or two or to eat lunch with the children. This is a drop-in event. Family members join us when they're available. Sammy's mother arrives with her sister and the baby cousin whom we've heard so much about, the one who listens to Sammy as he reads.

I observe. Teddy is obviously thrilled to see his big cousin Sammy. He races to Sammy with arms outstretched, and Sammy reciprocates, lifting Teddy into the air. Sammy's classmates stop playing Red Light, Green Light to admire Teddy. Teddy toddles among the children, sits on laps, and laughs delightedly. I'm struck by the easy way Sammy shares his cousin with his classmates. His big smile shows his pride in Teddy and his pleasure that his classmates like Teddy, too.

The children sit on the field, watching the teachers do a relay race. We run to the base, put on a silly hat, a skirt, a frilly shirt, and outsized boots, run back to our team, take these things off, and pass them to the next person in line. The children laugh, cheer their teachers on, and enjoy the last minutes of field day. I look at my students and notice Sammy right in the middle of the group, leaning against Paul, sharing his ice pop with Juan. He has made such progress with friends.

From my journal, May 15:

Field day, with its multiple changes—a new station every seven minutes, messy and exciting games, many visitors—is a fun day but a day with special challenges for a child who struggles with self-control. It can become overstimulating for such children. The way we set up field day provided Sammy with some of the structures he still needs: I was with the group all day to remind, redirect, and reinforce. There were no situations where he had to maintain control in a small group without adult guidance. On the other hand, it was hot, noisy, and full of materials that one might fling. Despite our emphasis on cooperation rather than competition, there were plenty of chances for children to irritate each other with cutting in line, insults to members of the opposing team of the moment, or other small moments of flaring antagonism. But Sammy came through field day with flying colors. He remained in control, shared his baby cousin, and had fun with classmates.

Dear Fourth Grade Teacher: "In third grade I learned to be an efficient problem-solver."

The children create a final portfolio to send on to their fourth grade teacher. I watch as Sammy looks carefully at each math paper. He pulls out samples of problem-solving, fractions, and geometry. He writes on his index cards legibly. "In third grade I learned to be an efficient problem-solver."

Next he opens his reader's notebook and attaches a sticky note to an entry. "I don't like writing reader's responses but I wrote two sentences." He places another sticky note on the cover of the book that he wrote about, *Silver for General Washington.* "A+ book—exciting," he writes.

Later, when I meet with Sammy to go over his portfolio, we talk about his academic work this year. "You have become a writer, Sammy," I say. "Your *Bubbles the Fish* piece was funny and lively. Your writing makes sense, and you add plenty of details."

"It's still not my favorite subject," Sammy, in his ever-honest way, replies. "But I know that I've gotten to be a better writer," he concedes.

The final letter home

It's the last Friday of school, and the children are writing their final letter home. Sammy is at the computer, writing to Teddy. "Dear Teddy," he types. "I still don't like letters home but I can write them. In third grade you will learn to write too. I have learned to be efficient and I have made some friends."

Sammy continues to hold confidently to his convictions—"I still don't like letters home," yet he's adapted to school expectations—"I can write them." Isn't that what we want for all of our children, that they can be themselves and be able to function in a group?

As for friends, there it is—"I have made some friends." It took all year, but he now recognizes and can enjoy the fact that he has something he's been wanting so badly.

"We were one awesome community"

We sit in a circle on the rug. "We're going to create a memory book, a class book about our year," I explain to the students. "We'll start by listing the important things we did this year."

Children volunteer their favorites: our trips to the Nature Center, the trip to the Native American museum, the Fall Fun party, working with our first grade buddies. They add those iconic third grade skills learned, such as cursive writing and multiplication facts. Sammy reminds us about creating our own Native American museum, Jenny suggests our passion study. School subjects go on the list, too, such as writers' workshop, readers' workshop, math, science, and social studies. I write each idea on chart paper.

Each child chooses one topic from the list to write about. I'm not surprised that Sammy chooses our town history walk. It was about history and it involved continuous movement.

As he composes, I remember how reluctant he was in September to write even one word. He especially didn't want to ruin his favorite subject, history, by writing about it. Now he writes, "We saw authentic costumes, actual clothes that people wore in the 1770s. They were fragile. None of us touched them."

The pages typed, the children illustrate their pages with black line drawings. I add my page, a poem to the class. Zoe suggests a title, *The Best Year for Our Community,* and all the students spontaneously show agreement with thumbs up. I photocopy the entire book so everyone has a copy.

We gather again on the rug, and I read the book aloud to the class. The group is quiet when I finish, thinking about our year. Sammy breaks the silence by saying, "We were one awesome community."

For some children, the first six weeks of school go on all year

I sit in the empty classroom, surrounded by handmade cards, flowers picked from backyard gardens, and my memories of the year. It's the last day of school, and the children have left for the summer. Next fall this classroom will be filled with a new group of children with their own strengths, struggles, and joys. For now, I think about this year, its children, its events, its accomplishments, and its unachieved goals.

I think about Sammy. He grew so, academically and socially. My efforts to support that growth continued up until the last minute of the last day. I reflect on some words from my friend and mentor Ruth Charney. One year when my class was struggling with issues of kindness and community, I wrote to Ruth frequently, often desperately. Ruth's wise response was that even after knowing we need to spend the first six weeks or so of school deliberately teaching children expected behaviors, we need to remember that sometimes these "first six weeks" take six months. Sometimes, for some children, I muse, the first six weeks take all year and even beyond. Today I'll be having lunch with Sammy's fourth grade teacher, to pass on some of the strategies that helped Sammy this year. I know she'll be there for him next year, facilitating his continued growth.

Sammy's written me a thank-you note, carefully inscribed in his best cursive. "Thank you for helping me in the friends department," it says. He grew as a student: Where he refused to write in September, now he writes with humor and grace. Where his math work was once confused and confusing, now it's efficient and clear. But what mattered to Sammy was friends. We all need to feel that people care about us, that we belong. Sammy needed lots of extra help to learn how to get along with other children. There's still plenty of room for growth, but he's on his way in this vital part of life.

I reread the note that Sammy's mom sent me this morning. "Thank you for such a fabulous year," she writes. "Sammy has grown socially, emotionally, and academically. It wasn't always easy, but under your watch I knew it would be OK. You always had time to help Sammy. You created such a supportive classroom. I know you were there for every other student, just the way you were for Sammy."

She's right—it was always OK. We didn't achieve impossible perfection, but Sammy grew as a student and as a group member. OK was enough. He'll go on to fourth grade, and another teacher will help him continue to grow. My other students grew as well, each of them in their own way. We cared about each other. We were a community of learners.

Epilogue

Sammy and I made great progress in our year together. We didn't achieve perfection, of course. It would have been unrealistic to expect that. We humans, after all, are only human. My colleagues, Sammy's subsequent teachers, took up their work with Sammy where I left off. He continued to progress socially, emotionally, and academically.

Over the ensuing years I saw Sammy occasionally, in the halls at school, in the supermarket, even once at a movie. Each time I ran into him, I noticed increased poise and confidence. "How are you, Ms. Crowe?" he would ask politely. I kept in touch with Sammy's mother, sometimes running into her while shopping or doing an errand, and sometimes contacting her deliberately with a quick email asking how Sammy was doing.

"Life's never easy with Sammy," she replied once. "But he's getting more mature. He has more self-control and self-awareness now. Of course, he's still his unique self!"

Friendships continued to be an issue for Sammy. "He has trouble reading social cues and he knows it," his mother said to me once. On the other hand, with increasing self-awareness, he learned to compensate—for example, by planning ahead of time whom to eat with to better navigate the social minefield that middle school lunch can be.

Though he continued to long for that one best friend, Sammy built a network of peers who enjoyed and looked out for him. When I dropped by his middle school, several friends hurried to find Sammy. "Ms. Crowe's here. Come and see her," they urged him.

It was several years before he learned to manage his organizational issues. His upper elementary and middle school teachers devoted time and energy to helping him maintain his assignment book. Now that he's in high school he's mastered the art of keeping track of assignments and deadlines.

In high school he's in the theater club and has a close circle of friends who share his interests and concerns. He hopes to go to college and is planning on majoring in history, of course.

Acknowledgments

I began my career as a preschool teacher. The foundation of early childhood education is careful observation of children. Without the skills of observation that I learned from my many early childhood colleagues, this book would not have been possible. I'd especially like to thank Dr. Michele Hoffnung and Dr. Clarice Pollack for guidance in honing my skills of careful noticing and reflection during those years. Dorothy H. Cohen and Virginia Stern's book *Observing and Recording the Behavior of Young Children* was a vital resource at that time. Without all that I learned from their thinking, this would have been a very different book.

Lucille Murray, my principal at Greeley School in Winnetka, Illinois, helped me to see how the skills of being an observant and reflective practitioner translated to a public elementary school environment.

School psychologists over the years have taught me how to see each child. I would especially like to recognize Margo Kohorn, Jack Bestor, Fred Rapchinsky, and Valerie Babich for so many things that I learned from them.

My colleagues in the teacher-research group at Coleytown Elementary School in Westport, Connecticut, helped me to develop my skills of reflection, supporting me in my journey to tailor my teaching strategies to the individuals in the class. I'd especially like to thank two members of that group: my long-term mentor Jane Fraser as well as the ever insightful Donna Skolnick.

My dear teaching friend Sarah Merriman Spencer as well as my team at Kings Highway School—Michele Cunningham, Kelly Harrison, Carmela DiStasio, Deborah Philips, and Jessica Carey—showed me how to collaborate in order to individualize teaching strategies for each student.

My work with Sammy, as well as my work with many other children like Sammy, was facilitated by numerous colleagues. Administrators, school psychologists, speech and language therapists, special educators, and teaching colleagues all helped. It takes a schoolwide community to effectively teach a child.

Vivian Gussin Paley's books have been among my favorite reads for many years. Before writing this book I reread all of them. I cannot understate my debt to her for leading the way in sharing thoughts about teaching by reflecting about one child.

The *Responsive Classroom* approach has guided me in creating safe and joyful classrooms where students like Sammy have the support that they need to thrive.

Many people at Northeast Foundation for Children, the organization behind the *Responsive Classroom* approach, helped turn this book from an idea into a reality. Executive Director Roxann Kriete and Director of Communications Mary Beth Forton recognized the potential in Sammy's story and invited me to write this book. I'm grateful that they gave me the opportunity. My editor, the incomparable Alice Yang, has been my companion and guide along the path to learning to write about teaching, learning, and children. Thank you, Alice. I also want to thank Paula Denton and Phil Pohlmeyer for giving feedback on the manuscript and Helen Merena for designing the book.

Jerry Allison, my life partner, has cheered me on, brought me cups of coffee, and told me when it was time to take a break and go climbing. Thank you, Jerry, for your unfailing support and understanding.

Without the support of Sammy and his family, this book would still be an idea rather than a reality. I would like to thank them for allowing me to share sometimes sensitive details about their lives. Their generosity was motivated by concern for all children.

Resources for Further Learning

The following strategies are all part of a research-backed approach to elementary teaching from Northeast Foundation for Children, Inc., called the *Responsive Classroom*® approach. Guided by the work of educational theorists and the experiences of practicing classroom teachers, the *Responsive Classroom* approach emphasizes social, emotional, and academic growth in a strong and safe school community. The goal is to enable optimal student learning.

Examples of these strategies can be found throughout this book.

CHILD DEVELOPMENT CONSIDERATIONS: Understanding children's developmental characteristics at different ages and using that knowledge to shape teaching so children can learn at their best

> *What Every 2nd Grade Teacher Needs to Know About Setting Up and Running a Classroom* by Margaret Berry Wilson. August 2010.
>
> *What Every 4th Grade Teacher Needs to Know About Setting Up and Running a Classroom* by Mike Anderson. August 2010.
>
> *Yardsticks: Children in the Classroom Ages 4–14*, 3rd ed., by Chip Wood. 2007.

MORNING MEETING: Gathering as a whole class each morning to greet one another, share news, and warm up for the day ahead

> *99 Activities and Greetings: Great for Morning Meeting … and other meetings, too!* by Melissa Correa-Connolly. 2004.
>
> *Morning Meeting Activities in a Responsive Classroom*®, DVD. 2008.
>
> *The Morning Meeting Book* by Roxann Kriete with contributions by Lynn Bechtel. 2002.
>
> *Morning Meeting Greetings in a Responsive Classroom*®, DVD. 2008.
>
> *Morning Meeting Messages K–6: 180 Sample Charts from Three Classrooms* by Rosalea S. Fisher, Eric Henry, and Deborah Porter, with an introduction by Marlynn K. Clayton. 2006.
>
> *Sample Morning Meetings in a Responsive Classroom*®, DVD and viewing guide. 2009.

RULE CREATION: Helping students create classroom rules to ensure an environment that allows all class members to meet their learning goals

Creating Rules with Students in a Responsive Classroom®, DVD. 2007.

Rules in School by Kathryn Brady, Mary Beth Forton, Deborah Porter, and Chip Wood. 2003.

INTERACTIVE MODELING: Teaching children to notice and internalize expected behaviors through a unique modeling technique

Rules in School by Kathryn Brady, Mary Beth Forton, Deborah Porter, and Chip Wood. 2003.

Teaching Children to Care: Classroom Management for Ethical and Academic Growth K–8 by Ruth Sidney Charney. 2002.

What Every 2nd Grade Teacher Needs to Know About Setting Up and Running a Classroom by Margaret Berry Wilson. August 2010.

What Every 4th Grade Teacher Needs to Know About Setting Up and Running a Classroom by Mike Anderson. August 2010.

REINFORCING, REMINDING, AND REDIRECTING LANGUAGE: Examples of ways to use words and tone as a tool to promote children's active learning, sense of community, and self-discipline

The Power of Our Words: Teacher Language that Helps Children Learn by Paula Denton, EdD. 2007.

Teacher Language in a Responsive Classroom®, DVD. 2009.

"TAKE A BREAK" AND OTHER STRATEGIES FOR RESTORING POSITIVE BEHAVIOR: Stopping misbehavior quickly and respectfully so that positive behaviors are restored

Rules in School by Kathryn Brady, Mary Beth Forton, Deborah Porter, and Chip Wood. 2003.

Solving Thorny Behavior Problems: How Teachers and Students Can Work Together by Caltha Crowe. 2009.

Teaching Children to Care: Classroom Management for Ethical and Academic Growth K–8 by Ruth Sidney Charney. 2002.

Time-Out in a Responsive Classroom®, DVD. 2007.

GUIDED DISCOVERY: Introducing classroom materials using a format that encourages independence, creativity, and responsibility

> *The First Six Weeks of School* by Paula Denton and Roxann Kriete. 2000.
>
> *Guided Discovery in a Responsive Classroom®*, DVD. 2010.
>
> *Teaching Children to Care: Classroom Management for Ethical and Academic Growth K–8* by Ruth Sidney Charney. 2002.

ACADEMIC CHOICE: Increasing student learning by allowing students teacher-structured choices in their work

> *Learning Through Academic Choice* by Paula Denton, EdD. 2005.

CLASSROOM ORGANIZATION: Setting up the physical room in ways that encourage students' independence, cooperation, and productivity

> *Classroom Spaces That Work* by Marlynn K. Clayton with Mary Beth Forton. 2001.
>
> *What Every 2nd Grade Teacher Needs to Know About Setting Up and Running a Classroom* by Margaret Berry Wilson. August 2010.
>
> *What Every 4th Grade Teacher Needs to Know About Setting Up and Running a Classroom* by Mike Anderson. August 2010.

WORKING WITH FAMILIES: Creating avenues for hearing parents' insights and helping them understand the school's teaching approaches

> *Parents & Teachers Working Together* by Carol Davis and Alice Yang. 2005.
>
> *What Every 2nd Grade Teacher Needs to Know About Setting Up and Running a Classroom* by Margaret Berry Wilson. August 2010.
>
> *What Every 4th Grade Teacher Needs to Know About Setting Up and Running a Classroom* by Mike Anderson. August 2010.
>
> *Yardsticks: Children in the Classroom Ages 4–14,* 3rd ed., by Chip Wood. 2007.

PROBLEM-SOLVING CONFERENCES, ROLE-PLAYING, AND OTHER COLLABORA-TIVE PROBLEM-SOLVING STRATEGIES: Engaging students in actively solving their common problems, from arguing and excluding classmates to refusing to do work

> *Solving Thorny Behavior Problems: How Teachers and Students Can Work Together* by Caltha Crowe. 2009.

> *Teaching Children to Care: Classroom Management for Ethical and Academic Growth K–8* by Ruth Sidney Charney. 2002.

All of these resources are published by Northeast Foundation for Children, Inc. and may be ordered from www.responsiveclassroom.org/bookstore.

CONSULTING SERVICES: Northeast Foundation for Children also provides consulting services to schools and a variety of professional development workshops on the *Responsive Classroom* approach for classroom teachers, teacher leaders, and administrators.

To learn more, visit www.responsiveclassroom.org.

Responsive ☀ Classroom®

Northeast Foundation for Children, Inc.
85 Avenue A, Suite 204, P. O. Box 718
Turners Falls, Massachusetts 01376-0718

800-360-6332   www.responsiveclassroom.org
info@responsiveclassroom.org

About the Author

Since beginning her teaching career thirty-eight years ago, Caltha Crowe has taught a range of elementary grades and preschool in a variety of settings, including schools in inner city New Haven, Connecticut, in the Chicago suburbs of Winnetka and Glencoe, and in Westport, Connecticut. Caltha has been involved with Connecticut's Beginning Educator Support and Training (BEST) program since its inception more than twenty years ago, serving as a mentor to new teachers, helping with mentor training, and serving on program advisory groups. A *Responsive Classroom*® consulting teacher, Caltha travels around the country to present workshops and coach teachers on using the *Responsive Classroom* approach. Caltha has a BA from Smith College, a master's degree in early childhood education from Goddard College, and a master's degree in educational leadership from Bank Street College of Education.